Kumihimo Jewelry
SIMPLIFIED

Learn to Braid with a Kumihimo Disk

Rebecca Ann Combs

KALMBACH BOOKS

Waukesha, Wisconsin

Dedication

To my friend and assistant store manager,
Alex Du Pont. This book wouldn't have been
possible without you. You're awesome!
Thanks for stepping up!

Kalmbach Books
21027 Crossroads Circle
Waukesha, Wisconsin 53186
www.JewelryAndBeadingStore.com

Published in 2016
20 19 18 17 16   1 2 3 4 5

Manufactured in the United States of America

ISBN: 978-1-62700-227-1
EISBN: 978-1-62700-228-8

Editor: Erica Swanson
Book Design: Lisa Schroeder
Illustrator: Kellie Jaeger
Photographer: William Zuback

Library of Congress Control Number: 2015960632

Contents

Introduction

Kumihimo is proving to be much more than a trend. It's a new category of jewelry making. As more and more people discover kumihimo, the demand increases for different styles of kumihimo jewelry projects. When I was asked to write a second beginner-friendly kumihimo book, I knew my challenge would be to keep it accessible to first-time braiders, while making it fresh and exciting for returning fans of *Kumihimo Basics & Beyond*. I have kept these two concepts at the top of my mind throughout the writing process.

To my new readers: Welcome! You're going to love kumihimo! The movements are rhythmic and repetitive, allowing you to focus solely on your braid while the rest of your thoughts drift away. All of the information you need to get started making kumihimo jewelry is here for you. I'll walk you step-by-step through your first project—from measuring and cutting the cords, to learning the braiding moves, to transforming your beautiful braid into a wonderful piece of jewelry you'll be proud to wear. You'll learn new skills and become more confident with every project. Take your time and enjoy the journey. I've included trouble-shooting sections as well, which will guide you through every potential stumbling block.

To my returning fans: Welcome back! We've been having so much fun braiding together and I know you're eager for more! This book is for you. Whereas my first book focuses entirely on the basic round braid (also called *kongoh gumi*), this book explores five different braid structures: basketweave, half-round, square, hollow, and trapezoid. In addition to the variety of braid forms, I'm very excited to add in some creative closures: projects that feature unique ways of finishing off braids besides the usual glue-on endcap. I think you'll have a lot of fun with these!

— *Rebecca Ann Combs*

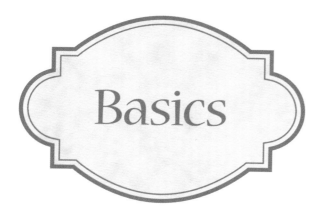

Basics

What is Kumihimo?

Kumihimo is traditional Japanese braiding. The techniques go back thousands of years, but the heyday of kumihimo in Japan was during the time of the samurai. The word kumihimo comes from the Japanese terms for gathering or combining threads. It is the name of the technique and also refers to the resulting braid. Next time you're at an art museum with a good Asian art collection, look closely at the samurai armor. Notice the little braids that lace the different sections together: That's kumihimo. You'll also see braids used as adornment covering large sections of the armor.

While the samurai are long gone, kumihimo continues on. These days in Japan, you'll find kumihimo used for decorative and ceremonial pulls and tassels, embellishments for clothing, *obi jime* (that's the belt that ties a kimono shut), and in recent years, jewelry and fashion accessories. With the techniques learned in this book you could make any of those things, but we'll focus on making jewelry.

How to Use This Book

There are five different braid structures taught in this book: three eight-warp braids (basketweave, half-round, and square) and two 16-warp braids (hollow and trapezoid). Be sure to master the eight-warp braids before moving onto the 16-warp braids. The projects in each chapter are arranged in a skill-building sequence. The first project introduces the new braid. Spend some time here and really get comfortable with the braid before moving on to the next project. Subsequent projects add new skills, techniques, and design concepts by building on what was previously learned. I highly recommend that you start at the beginning and work your way through. Even if you're not going to make a project, read through it so you don't miss out on any new information.

What about those numbers? The numbers on the disk are a convenient way to communicate a braiding sequence. When I teach a kumihimo class, we focus on how and where the cords are moving rather than trying to memorize the list of numbers; however, many people find the numbers helpful when getting started with a new braid.

In my first book, I taught the projects without using the numbers because the basic round braid (kongoh gumi) rotates around the disk and the series of numbers is too long to be useful. For the braids in this book, we reset the disk after every sequence, making our list of numbers shorter and more manageable; however, you still don't need to memorize them. They're just for reference.

The numbers are helpful to some people and a distraction to others. If you don't like the numbers, you can always flip the disk over and work on the blank side. Just transfer the dots so you have some reference points.

Kumihimo Toolkit

You just need a few basic tools to get started making kumihimo jewelry. Gather them together and keep them handy as you work your way through this book. You'll need these tools for every project.

Kumihimo Disk

You'll want at least two disks in your toolbox: one standard thickness and one double thickness. Each project will list the recommended disk thickness. Disks are inexpensive and it's nice to have some extras so you can have multiple projects going at once.

There are more varieties of kumihimo disks on the market today than ever before! This is great news because you can choose the disk that is most comfortable and is best suited for your favorite braiding materials.

Diameter: Standard diameters are generally 4" or 6". The diameter of a disk is a matter of personal preference. It doesn't have any effect on the finished braid, but for some projects, there is an advantage to using one diameter disk over the over. For example, you might find it more comfortable to learn 16-warp braids on a 6" disk because all of those bobbins will have a bit more room to spread out and will be less prone to tangling. Conversely, working on a 4" disk allows to you braid closer to the end of the warps and save on fiber waste.

Thickness: Standard thickness is ⅜". Up until recently, all kumihimo disks just came in this one thickness (more or less). Now there are double-thick disks available that are ¾" thick. These are helpful when working with thin or slippery fibers. The double thickness gives each slot more surface area with which to grip the fiber. The double-thick disk was extremely helpful to me when braiding the "Triple Threat Bracelet," p. 105, since it uses Soft Flex wire that is both thin and slippery. The downside to the double thickness is an extra center weight is required for braids that need downward tension to form correctly (for example, the basketweave and hollow braids). The supply list for each project lists the recommended disk thickness and center weight.

Quality: Quality varies from brand to brand. Look for dense foam that will hold up to repeated use and not bend too much when you're using weights.

Numbers: On the BeadSmith brand disk I used for the step-by-step photos, the numbers are printed to the right of the slot it refers to. This can vary by brand, so be sure you're clear on which number goes to which slot for your disk before you start a pattern.

Kumihimo disks

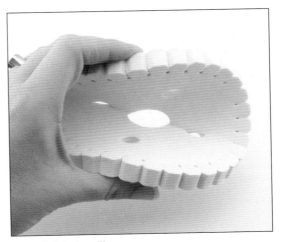

This disk is too flimsy.

Bobbins

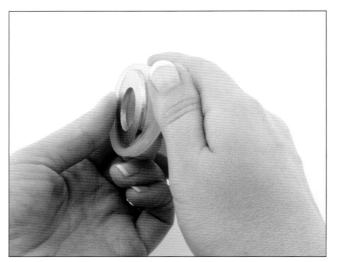
Weighted bobbins

Center weight

Bobbins

Bobbins are essential on all but the shortest of braids because they keep your braiding fibers tidy and tangle-free. The bobbins I like are made of a soft plastic and can be flipped open or closed by pushing on the domed side. When braiding, each fiber or group of fibers that share a bobbin is called a warp.

Weighted Bobbins

The standard thickness disk does a good job controlling the braid tension when working with warps 1mm or thicker. When I'm braiding with seed beads on thin warps, I use weighted bobbins so gravity can help hold everything in place and keep the warps from shifting around.

A few years back, the only option for weighted bobbins was to make them yourself by sanding the flat back of the bobbin and gluing on a heavy washer using a thick layer of E6000. I worked with BeadSmith to develop bobbins with built-in weights. They're ready to go right out of the package with no gluing required. You can pop the weights out of these bobbins when your project calls for plain bobbins. Just open the bobbin and pull against the plastic lip holding the weight in place. The weights pop right back in when you need them. Each weighted bobbin weighs about 23 grams.

Center Weight

Downward tension on the braid helps it form correctly. Using a clip-on weight is the easiest, most reliable way to achieve this. I use a barrel-shaped weight with an attached alligator clip.

These are sometimes sold under the names "Kumihimo Weights" or "Gator Weights." The smaller version is sometimes called "Lite" and weighs about 45 grams. The larger one is sometimes called "heavy" or "regular" and weighs about 90 grams. How much center weight you need depends on which braid structure you're doing and what materials you're using. Each project supply list will give the recommended weight size. When experimenting with your own designs, keep in mind that a heavier center weight makes a looser braid.

Wait a minute! Shouldn't a heavier weight make my braid tighter? Let's think about what the center weight is doing to the braid. It's pulling the point of braiding down through the hole. The lower the point of braiding, the more fiber is used with every move. Using more fiber each move results in a longer stitch and a looser braid.

Needles

You'll use needles for two different jobs: picking up beads and sewing through braids. For picking up beads, my favorite needle is a big-eye needle. It's essentially two thin, flexible pieces of metal soldered together at each end, creating an eye that runs the entire length of the needle. Nylon braiding string passes easily through this large eye and makes stringing beads a snap.

When you need to sew through a thick braid, you want a strong needle with a bit of flex to it that won't bend in half easily. For this job, I prefer Tulip brand beading needles (size 10) because they're easy to thread and hard to break. For your projects, you can use any size 10 beading needle.

Scissors
Choose strong, sharp fabric scissors that will cut cleanly through multiple cords at once.

Your first braid is going to be 8mm thick, so you'll want plenty of cutting power to slice through the braid in a single cut—no hacking!

You'll also want some basic craft scissors to cut fiber and wire.

Binding Thread
Before you can cut a braid into pieces, you'll need to bind it so the cut end doesn't unravel. To bind my pieces, I use regular beading thread, such as Nymo, One-G, or KO.

If you're gluing on an endcap, the color of the thread doesn't matter because it will be covered. Otherwise, try to match the color of the thread to the braid.

Glue
Some jewelers don't trust glue because they don't believe that it will hold. I think this distrust comes from not allowing the glue to cure properly. I use E6000 whenever I need to glue an endcap and it's never let me down; however, it does take 24 hours to cure fully. Don't glue on your endcaps and come back in a few hours to check on the braid. If you pull off the partially set endcap and then stick it back on again, the glue will never cure as it should (this is where glue failure comes from). When you allow the E6000 to set up undisturbed for 24 hours, it's incredibly strong and reliable. In addition, it's waterproof, dries clear, and doesn't bond to skin.

Be sure to buy your E6000 in a small tube. It has a relatively short shelf life once the container has been opened.

You'll also be using a jeweler's glue called Hypo Cement for some projects. Hypo Cement is much thinner than E6000 and comes with a needle-tipped applicator so you can put it right where you want it. Use Hypo Cement for gluing knots and other detail work, but it's not strong enough for weight-bearing applications, like gluing endcaps.

For some projects, white craft glue (like Elmer's) is helpful for stiffening the ends of cords.

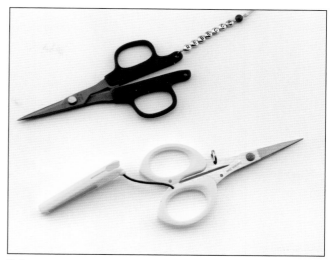
Scissors

Binding thread

Beading thread

Jewelry pliers

Toothpick
It may sound trivial, but a toothpick is the secret to precision E6000 application.

Scrap Paper
Like the toothpick, scrap paper could easily be overlooked—but when it comes time to glue, your work surface will thank you.

Measuring Tape
You'll be measuring quite a bit working on these kumihimo projects: measuring out warps before you start, measuring the braid as you work, and measuring your own wrist to ensure the perfect fit.

Jewelry Pliers
These aren't needed at all for the braiding portion of the projects, but you'll need some handy when it comes time to add the clasp. I like to use one pair of bentnose pliers and one pair of chainnose pliers to open and close jump rings, but any combination of pliers is fine. You'll also need roundnose pliers for making wire-wrapped endcaps. I like to dip my flatnose and bentnose pliers in Tool Magic (liquid rubber) to help prevent scratching my jump rings or wire.

Wire Cutters
Again, you won't need these for every project, but they're essential for snipping the excess wire after making a wrapped loop on a cone or for making your own custom endcap.

Calipers
The supply list for each project tells you what size endcap you'll need, but once you start to venture on your own and change the recipes, you'll need calipers to measure the diameter of your braids. Look for one that measures in millimeters because that's how most endcaps come labeled. If you can find one with both metric and English measurements, even better. My preferred calipers are digital for easy reading. They switch between metric and English with the push of a button, and measure both inside and outside diameter.

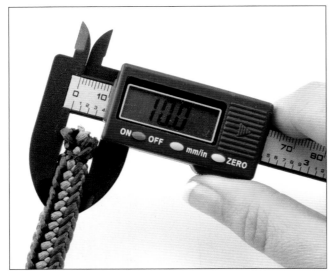

Calipers

Braiding Fibers and Other Supplies

You'll be pleased to know you can make kumihimo braids with pretty much anything you can get your hands on: cording of all sorts, ribbon, yarn, embroidery floss, leather, silk, wire, etc.

Satin Cord

My favorite satin cord goes by the brand name Rattail™ and is composed of rayon over a cotton core. It is my recommended fiber for a first braid. This American-made fiber is silky smooth with a lustrous finish and comes in lots of colors. It's also very easy to work with and widely available. Rattail™ is available in three sizes, but the naming can be a bit confusing. The manufacturer calls the sizes #0, #1, and #2 (smallest to largest), but the major distributors call the sizes 1mm, 2mm, and 3mm. I've also heard the various sizes called *bug-tail*, *mouse-tail*, and *rattail*. These cord sizes are generally .7–1mm for the small, 1.3–1.5mm for the medium, and 2–2.2mm for the large.

I refer to the sizes as 1mm, 2mm, and 3mm in the book, as this is how they are most often labeled in bead stores. Rattail™ is commonly available in over 40 different solid colors, and some ribbon dyers offer it in an ever-changing rainbow of hand-dyed variegated colors.

You'll also find Chinese-made nylon satin cord. It's a little cheaper, but the texture is stiffer and less silky. It also tends to braid up thicker than the corresponding size in rayon.

Satin cord

Medium

Small

Large

Twisted Nylon Braiding String

This is one of my most commonly used braiding fibers when doing beaded kumihimo and is my new favorite fiber for micro braiding. C-Lon and Superlon (S-Lon) are the two most common brand names. Look for the words "cord" or "string" when shopping for these. C-Lon and S-Lon both make a "thread" size that is too thin for braiding with and is better suited as a binding thread. The cord comes in four sizes: Micro Cord (.12mm), Fine Tex-135 (.4mm), Size 18 (.5mm), and Tex-400 (.7mm). You'll mostly use size 18 in this book.

Leather

I really enjoy braiding with leather because it dramatically changes the look of a braid and adds interesting negative space to a design. Quality matters; weak spots can snap, so inspect the leather to make sure it has uniform thickness. I used 1.5mm Greek leather, as well as suede deerskin lace for projects in this book.

Twisted nylon braiding string

Leather

Ribbon

This is a fun category to play with because ribbon is available in such a wide range of diameters, fabrics, and finishes, it's difficult to make blanket statements about the braids you might make with this versatile fiber. One important thing to keep in mind is ribbon often condenses or twists as you work, and the finished braid sometimes looks very different from the starting material.

Embroidery Floss and Pearl Cotton

Both of these materials are inexpensive and easy to find. Available in many colors, embroidery floss and pearl cotton are good choices when you want a braid a little more casual and more "friendship bracelet" in appearance.

Endcaps and Cones

Endcaps are the easiest and most common way to finish off kumihimo jewelry. An endcap is basically a hollow tube, generally made of metal, that is capped off at one end and ideally has a loop attached. Cones are another great way to finish off a braid, but because the end of the cone is open, you have to do a little wire wrapping before you use them.

Both cones and endcaps are available in a wide range of sizes and colors. The projects in this book all specify what size endcap you'll need, but once you start venturing beyond the supply list, you'll need to figure that out on your own. The easiest thing to do is measure the diameter of the braid using calipers. When measuring with the calipers, it is important not to squeeze the braid too tightly or you'll get an inaccurate reading. Say you measure your braid and get a reading of 4.5mm. What does that mean? A 5mm endcap will be a perfect fit, a 6mm endcap will be a comfortable fit, and maybe you can squeeze it into a 4mm endcap if you're really determined and you bind the braid very tightly. When shopping for endcaps and cones, remember the inside diameter is the measurement that matters. Some cones and endcaps come labeled with the outside diameter.

Seed Beads

Seed beads come in an astounding array of colors and finishes. They're available in a variety of sizes from the teeny-tiny size 15° to the not-so-small size 3°. Choose round beads for a smooth braid or experiment with hexes or triangles for faceted flair. Japanese seed beads are the most uniform in size and shape and are my favorite type of seed beads. I've also braided successfully with Czech seed beads, but they tend to vary greatly in size. Some beads will be thick and tall, while others are flat little donuts. You can either cull the funny sized beads at the beginning or just ignore the difference and enjoy the texture it brings to your project. I recommend avoiding Chinese seed beads because the holes tend to be roughly finished and can cut through your stringing material.

Ribbon

Endcaps and cones

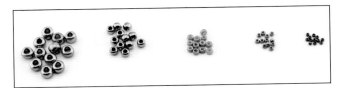

Seed beads

Kumihimo Math

Before you begin any kumihimo project, you must first decide on your desired finished length. What are you making? A bracelet? A necklace? A belt? You must have a number in mind because you cannot add more thread or cord to your project once started. This isn't like knitting or crochet where you can tie on or splice in additional thread. You must cut as much fiber as you'll need for your entire project at the beginning. Fear not! There's an easy-to-remember ratio: **You need three times your finished length per warp.**

For example: Let's say you want to make an 18" necklace. $18 \times 3 = 54$. That means you need 54" for each of the eight warps of the braid. (Remember that when braiding, each fiber or group of fibers that share a bobbin is called a warp.) 54" is 1½ yd. 1½ yd. x 8 = 12. That means you need 12 yd. total for the 18" necklace using an eight-warp braid structure.

Because I can't add more to the project once started, I use a ratio that's actually pretty generous. Nothing is sadder than running out of cord when you're just a bit short of your target length. The actual amount of material needed will depend on its thickness and the braid structure. Thinner cords have less "up take" than thicker cords. Individual braiders will also braid with varying tensions and will require differing material allowances; however, if you follow the 3-to-1 rule, you shouldn't come up short.

If you're concerned about being frugal with your materials, take good notes about your braiding. Before starting a project, jot down what type of fiber you're using and how much was cut for each warp. When you're finished, record the final braid length. With that information, you can calculate your own personal usage ratio for each type of material and braid structure.

Length and Fit

Some of these kumihimo projects can be quite thick—up to ½" in diameter. Allow about 15–20 percent extra length to ensure that thick necklaces fit you the way you like. This is even more of an issue with bracelets because of the small circumference. For example, the "Ombraid" (p. 86) is just under ½" thick and about 8" long, but it fits a 6" wrist.

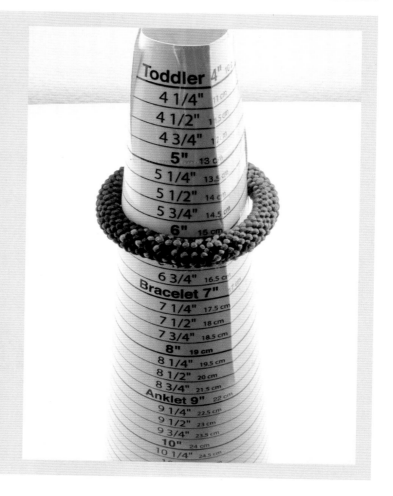

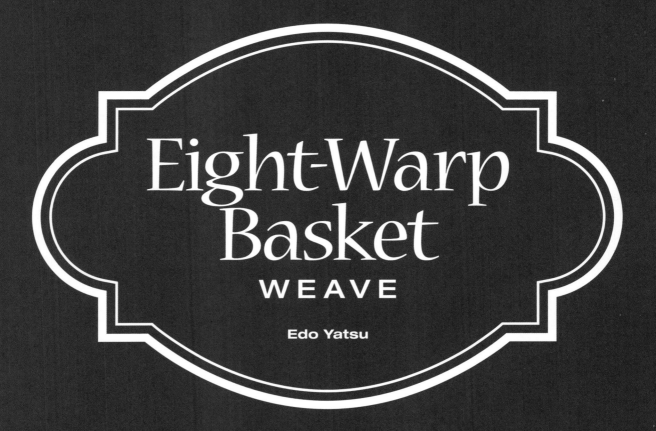

Eight-Warp Basket
WEAVE

Edo Yatsu

This braid is known as basket weave kumihimo because of the over-under pattern of the warps. You might also hear it called the *hollow braid* from time to time— that's because the warps never cross the center of the point of braiding, resulting in a small hole in the middle. With eight warps, the braid is still firm and self-supporting, but later in the book you'll learn a related 16-warp structure that is truly hollow.

It's possible to incorporate beads into a basketweave braid. As you'll see with "In the Loop Bracelet" and "Pirouette Necklace," the beads sit at a 45-degree angle to the braid, giving your beaded jewelry fabulous texture.

This braid structure is called *Edo Yatsu* in Japanese. *Edo* was the former name for Tokyo and *Yatsu* means eight. So this is an eight-warp braid from Edo.

Double-Take
Necklace

In this project, you'll learn the basic skills needed to complete all of the projects in this book: how to set up the disk, how to manage your center-weight, how to spot and fix mistakes, and how to transform your braid into jewelry. Master this project. Learn it forwards and backwards. Then you'll be ready to take the next step on your kumihimo journey.

When learning the basketweave braid, it's easiest to see the pattern when you use two colors. You may be looking at the finished necklace and thinking, "Hey! She used more than two colors! Why can't I?" Well, I cheated a bit. My necklace is mostly two colors: black (A) and pink-ish (B). For the pink-ish I used two cranberry, one strawberry, and one dusty plum. Feel free to do the same where you choose all one solid color for your color A warps and several shades or tints of a different color for your B warps. Just make sure you can easily distinguish between your As and your Bs. I chose high-contrast purple and turquoise for the step-by-step photos to make it easier for you to see.

➤ Supplies

Kumihimo Toolkit
- standard thickness disk
- **8** plain bobbins
- **90g** center weight

Other Materials
- 3mm satin cord
  - 6 yd. color A
  - 6 yd. color B
- pendant with a 10mm or larger bail
- 1 set 8mm (ID) magnetic endcaps

Finished Necklace Length: 18"

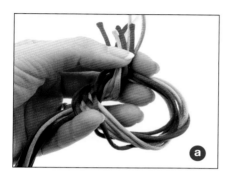

TIP
When you choose a pendant large enough to fit over the endcaps, you can swap it between braids of different colors.

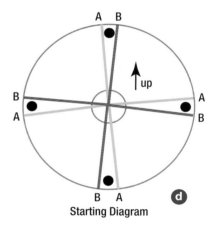

Starting Diagram

Set Up
Cut four 1½-yd. pieces of color A satin and four 1½-yd. pieces of color B satin. Bring the eight ends together so they're more or less even. Don't worry about this too much. Tie all eight cords together using an overhand knot. An overhand knot is where you make a loop and then bring the tails through the loop **(a)**. You want the knot fairly close to the end of the cords **(b)**.

I find it easiest to make a large loop and walk the knot towards the end of the cords rather than trying to make a small loop and knot right near the end.

Take a look at the kumihimo disk. Notice the four black dots. These are there to help us evenly space the cords

during set up and to keep us on track while we're braiding. For this braid, and for all the braids in this book, it's important to keep track of which side of the disk is the top. Orient the disk so slots 32 and 1 are at the top and keep it in this position while you work. If you prefer to work without the numbers, transfer the four dots to the blank side of the disk and mark one side as up.

Position the knot so that it's in the middle of the hole in the disk **(c)**.

Lock one warp into every slot that is adjacent to a dot. That's one cord per slot—no sharing. Your colors should be alternating around the disk. Match yours to the starting diagram **(d)**.

Ready to braid!

32 → 7

8 → 15

It doesn't matter if the cords are crossing funny or somewhat jumbled looking. Relax… Anything you don't like at the beginning of the braid can be cut off when you finish.

TIP
When reading kumihimo patterns, the top position (farthest from your body) is called north. The bottom position (closest to your body) is called south. Left is west and right is east.

With these long cords hanging down, you have a tangled mess waiting to happen. Bobbins to the rescue! Open the bobbins by gently bending back the domed side. Use your thumb to hold one of the loose cord ends against the flat inside of the bobbin. With your other hand, wind the cord onto the bobbin (e).

It doesn't matter if you wind towards you or away from you, but the more

TIPS FOR LEARNING THE BRAID
- **The braiding sequence is composed of two rounds: first clockwise, then counter-clockwise.**
- **Hang on tight if you get lost and don't set down the disk between moves! The next warp to move is always adjacent to the warp you just placed.**
- **Always reposition the warps before starting the next sequence.**

detail-oriented among us usually wind all eight in the same direction. Keep winding until the bobbin is about 1" below the disk, then pop the bobbin closed. As you braid, you'll discover the ideal length for you—but in general, the shorter you keep the warps, the less they spin around and tangle. Wind each of the eight cords onto a bobbin. Clip the center weight onto the knot below the disk (f).

Double-check your work: Each of the eight cords should be firmly locked into a slot. The cords are positioned so that

there is one pair straddling each of the four dots. The knot is centered in the hole and both it and the warps are flush with the surface of the disk. The center weight is clipped to the knot below the disk (g).

Perfect! This is the standard starting position for an eight-warp basketweave braid, as well as the eight-warp half-round braid. The arrangement of the colors will vary with other projects, but if I tell you to put the cords on the disk in the eight-warp standard starting position, this is what I'm talking about.

16 → 23

24 → 32

1 → 26

25 → 18

17 → 10

9 → 1

TIP

This color arrangement is ideal for learning the basketweave braid because each color only moves in one direction. In this example, the turquoise always moves clockwise and the purple always moves counter-clockwise.

Braiding

Work clockwise for the first round. Use your right hand to lift the top-left warp out of its slot (turquoise in the photos). Moving clockwise, jump over the neighboring warp and lock it in the slot right above the next group of warps **(h)**.

Use your right hand to pick up the adjacent warp; it's also turquoise. Moving clockwise, jump over the neighboring warp and lock in place to the right of the next group of warps **(i)**.

Use your right hand to hold the disk and use your left hand to pick up the next warp (also turquoise). Moving clockwise, jump one and lock it below the next group of warps **(j)**.

Use your left hand to pick up the adjacent warp; you guessed it—turquoise. Moving clockwise, jump one and lock it to the left of the top warp **(k)**. Now, complete the sequence by doing a round of counter-clockwise moves. Use your left hand to pick up the top-right warp (purple in the photos). Moving counter-clockwise, jump one and lock it above the next group of warps **(l)**.

Don't put it in the gap left during the last round. Use your left hand to pick up the adjacent warp; it's also purple. Moving counter-clockwise, jump one and lock it to the left of the next group of warps **(m)**.

Hold the disk with your left hand and use your right hand to pick up the next warp (also purple). Moving counter-clockwise, jump one and lock it below the next group of warps **(n)**.

Use your right hand to pick up the adjacent purple warp. Moving counter-clockwise, jump one and lock it to the right of the top warp **(o)**.

I stopped braiding in the middle of the sequence and forgot where I left off. Help!

Take a look at your braid and find the group of three warps. (If you only have groups of two warps, then you're at the beginning of a sequence.) This group of three indicates you just added a warp to this group. The middle warp needs to move next.

I forgot which way I'm moving. Should I go clockwise or counter-clockwise?

Take a look at the group of three warps. Is there a gap? If so, then you need to move counter-clockwise.

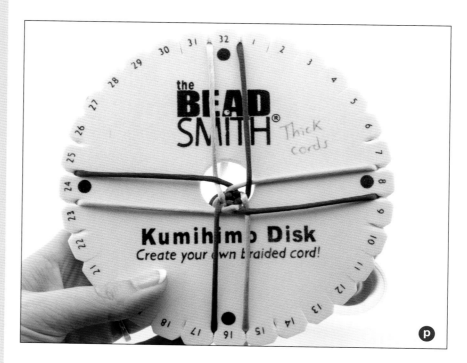

Move counter-clockwise.

Move clockwise.

Well done! You've completed the sequence: one round clockwise followed by one round counter-clockwise. Did you notice how all of the movements are essentially the same? A warp jumps over its neighboring warp and then joins the next group. This can be your braiding mantra for the basketweave braid: **"Jump over your neighbor and join the next group."**

Before we can continue braiding, we need to reset the disk to the starting position. The warps surrounding the top dot are fine. You can leave them alone, but notice there are two empty slots between the warps at the bottom and side dots. To reset, just scoot each warp one slot closer to the dot. Now it looks like the starting position again **(p)**.

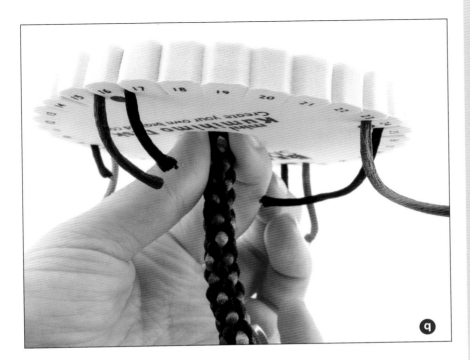

Repeat the braiding sequence a few hundred times, and pretty soon you'll have a braid. If you need to take a break from braiding, remember to stop after completing an entire sequence and repositioning so you can easily find your place when you return.

Finishing
Taking the Braid off of the Disk

You're nearing the end. Some or all of the bobbins have probably fallen off by now. Even if the braid looks long enough for your project, at this point you may as well use up all of the fiber. We'll cut the braid to the perfect length and any scrap braid can be added to your kumihimo notebook or possibly be made into a bracelet or keychain. Just keep braiding until one warp is too short to lock into a slot on the disk. (One warp always finishes before the others, no matter how evenly you cut them at the beginning. Even if your tension is perfectly even, one always comes up shorter than the rest. Don't sweat it.)

Now that you're finished braiding, remove any remaining bobbins. Holding the braid right below the disk, remove each of the eight warps from its slot **(q)**.

Tie all eight cords together using an overhand knot, just like at the beginning of the braid.

TROUBLESHOOTING

How do I know if my tension is ok?

For the most part, the foam disk does a great job of managing the tension for you. Because of the heavy weight clipped to the braid, the point of braiding (where all the cords intersect) tends to settle near the bottom of the hole. So long as the braid stays in one place and isn't jerking side to side with every move, then your tension is fine. If the warps are falling out of the slots, then the tension is too loose.

Even tension comes with practice. In the beginning, most people tend to pull harder on one side than the other. Be conscious of your movements, relax, and with time, it will even out. The basketweave braid has a gentle spiral to it, so don't obsess about trying to make the braid straight.

My braid is getting fatter and fatter! What's going on?

Make sure that your center weight isn't resting on your lap or the table while you work. If it's not hanging freely, then it's not doing its job. The basketweave braid requires strong downward tension to form correctly or it can braid around itself. Pull down on the braid and it will go back to normal. The braid will be a bit loose at this point. If a loose braid bothers you, unbraid to before that point and make sure the weight is dangling when you rebraid. As your braid gets longer, knot it to keep the length comfortable.

Two of the most common braiding mistakes

1. Braiding in the wrong direction: You did the clockwise moves fine. Then you got distracted and started doing the clockwise moves again without doing the counter-clockwise round.

You forgot to do the counter-clockwise moves.

2. Falling in the hole: When doing the counter-clockwise moves, it's tempting to place the warp into the hole vacated by the clockwise moves. Don't! Place the warp on the outside of the group.

The purple warp in the middle of the bottom should be placed to the left of the group.

I'm demonstrating the binding knot with satin cord so it's easier to see. You should use beading thread.

Binding

You now have a beautiful kumihimo braid, but it's not yet a necklace. To make the transformation, we need to add our endcaps, but first we have to do something about the huge knot at either end of the braid. We're going to have to cut the braid. Don't panic! I'll walk you through binding each end of the braid so it doesn't unravel when you cut it.

Before we bind the braid, let's give it a quick stretch. Take hold of the braid at either end and pull in opposite directions. The basketweave structure doesn't really have much stretch in it because we used the heavy weight while braiding, but it's a good practice to give all of your braids a tug before binding, just in case. This stretching process is called *relaxing the braid*. Once you've relaxed the braid, you shouldn't experience any further stretching unless you're braiding with a stretchy fiber. The satin cord is pretty good about holding its shape once relaxed, but you'll find some yarns (especially if you have a heavy pendant) just keep on stretching forever.

Now is a good time to have a look at the beginning of your braid. Any mistakes near the start that you'd like to cut off? Is it somewhat funny-looking near the knot? You decide where to place the bind. If your braid is perfect in every way right from the start, well done! You still can't bind too close to the knot. Be sure to leave yourself about ¼" gap between the knot and the binding so you have enough room to get the scissors in there.

Cut a piece of binding thread about 18" long. Fold it over so it's not quite in half. You want a long side and a short side. By folding it over, you've created a loop of thread. It's not twisted or wrapped or anything, but this little U-turn in the thread is our loop. Place the loop on top of the braid, parallel to the braid,

This is what the binding knot will look like when you use beading thread.

wherever you would like the binding to be. At this point, I generally transfer the braid to my non-dominant hand. I'm right-handed, so for me the knot is on the left and I'm holding the loop in place, just to the right of the knot, using my left hand **(r)**.

Use your dominant hand to wrap the longer piece of thread around the braid. The short piece of thread is sitting on top of the braid, so it gets covered by the wraps as well. Take your time with this and make it pretty neat. You want each wrap next to the wrap before—not on top of it. Keep it snug. Wrap around four or five times. If you prefer not to count, the wraps should be about ⅛" wide. Keep holding on to everything with your non-dominant hand and use your dominant hand to bring the working thread (it was the longer piece, but may be shorter now after wrapping) through the loop **(s)**.

Now grab the short tail (it's just been hanging out this whole time) and pull **(t)**.

Pulling the short tail closes the loop. Ta da! Now pull each thread in opposite

directions to tighten everything up **(u)**. Make an extra little square knot on top for good measure. Trim the thread tails as close as you can, but DON'T CUT THE BRAID YET **(v)**.

From this binding, measure to your desired necklace length and bind again. Be sure to account for the length of your endcaps and clasp. For example, I like my necklaces 18" long and I'm using a magnetic endcap that won't add any length, so my two bindings should be 18" apart. But if I wanted an 18" necklace with a toggle clasp, I would need to subtract the length of my clasp—usually about 1"—from my braid. In that case, I would make the two bindings 17" apart and the necklace would be 18" after I added the clasp.

A half inch down from the second binding, bind again. If the excess braid not needed for the necklace is long enough, it can be made into a bracelet. Whenever you want to cut the braid into two usable pieces, you need to make two bindings and cut between them **(w)**.

TROUBLESHOOTING

This doesn't look right. I think I made a mistake.

First of all, take a deep breath. It's going to be ok. If you have a mistake in your braid you have a couple options. First of all, you can ignore it. This is an especially appealing option if you're near the beginning or end of the braid. Any "oopsies" can always be cut off if your braid is long enough. If that's your choice, keep on braiding. If necessary, shift the warps so they're back to the starting position.

The second approach to dealing with a braiding error is to undo it and fix it. Unbraiding is just like braiding forward, except all of the moves are in reverse and it takes a lot more concentration. Turn the TV off for this part. Start by identifying where you left off and which direction you were traveling. Now that you know where you are, you're going to unbraid one warp at a time. If you're unbraiding from the start of a new sequence, remember to make the gaps on both sides and the bottom or you won't have room to place the warps as you unbraid.

! WARNING: DO NOT REMOVE MORE THAN ONE WARP AT A TIME. DO NOT TAKE ALL OF THE WARPS OFF THE DISK AND START MOVING THEM AROUND.

Leave it alone! No haircuts!

Cutting

Before you cut, it's important to gather all of the materials and tools you'll need for gluing. The little binding you made in the last step isn't really attached to the braid. If you cut the end off and then toss the braid in your "to be finished later" drawer, the binding can come right off the end of the braid.

Look at the bindings. For every bind there is a "keep" side and a "throw away" side. Be sure to cut on the "throw away" side, otherwise you'll cut the binding off. Using your best scissors, cut as near to the bind as possible without cutting through the binding **(x)**.

The most important thing about cutting is to be brave. Make one cut—no hacking or haircuts. Do this for each end of the necklace and the bracelet, if you're making one **(y)**.

Adding the Pendant

Some pendants have bails large enough to fit over the endcap; others do not. You need to find out before you glue the endcaps on. If the bail is too small to fit over the endcap, add the pendant **after** cutting off the knot, but **before** gluing on the endcap. If it's going to be a really tight squeeze getting the pendant onto the braid, consider smearing a tiny dab of glue onto the binding and letting it dry before stringing the pendant. This way the friction from the pendant doesn't pull the binding off.

Magnetic endcaps don't always open in the center. Check for a side seam **(z)**.

Unbraiding

Pay close attention while unbraiding. You're looking for the mistake so you can correct it. Once you've found it, unbraid one more sequence just to be sure. Then check your point of braiding to make sure it is correct. Starting with the top-left warp (32) and working clockwise, your warps should be arranged under, over, under, over, under, over, under, and over.

Gluing

When working with magnetic endcaps, it's important to observe which part of the endcap is magnetic and which part attaches to the braid. Failure to make this critical observation can result in the endcap being glued shut or attached backwards, which is no fun. Carefully separate the two sides of the endcap and set them on the table so the magnets are facing the table and the open braid end is pointing up **(aa)**.

I like to work over a small scrap of paper so I don't get glue on the table. Open the E6000 and squeeze a small, 4–5mm blob onto a toothpick. Use the toothpick to smear the glue around the inside of the endcap. You want the glue to cover the bottom and sides of the endcap so that it's about half full of glue **(bb)**.

Hold the braid still with one hand and use the other hand to slowly twist and push the endcap onto the braid. The more slowly you push, the more time the glue has to soak into the braid, resulting in less excess glue oozing out. If you do encounter an ooze situation, just take a clean toothpick and wipe the excess glue away **(cc)**.

If you do this right away, you'll notice the glue balls up like rubber cement and is very easy to remove. Now comes the hardest part: waiting. Once you have glued endcaps to each end of the necklace and bracelet, set everything aside and allow to dry for 24 hours.

TIP

You have noticed I wrote "thick cords" on my kumihimo disk. That's because thick cords like 3mm satin or leather stretch out the slots a bit. This way, I can have one disk reserved for thicker materials and my other disk for thin strings like we'll use in the next project.

Braiding with Beads

One of the first questions beaders ask when learning kumihimo is, "How can I add beads to this?" Of course slider beads and pendants can be added to any braid, but some braid patterns allow for beads to be worked right into the structure of the braid. We'll explore this with the basketweave and half-round braids. Be sure to make several fiber-focused braids without beads and practice unbraiding before moving onto the beaded projects.

Each braid structure has a particular way of locking the bead into place. For the basketweave braid, you alternate between adding and not adding a bead **(dd)**.

For the half-round braid, you tuck the bead under a perpendicular warp to lock it in place **(ee)**.

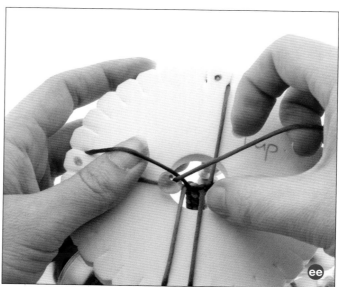

In the Loop
Bracelet

Creative Closure

With this project, you'll learn the basics of incorporating beads into a basketweave braid. The techniques learned in this project will also be used in the "Pirouette Necklace," p. 38, so pay special attention to locking the beads in place and the troubleshooting advice. This bracelet also features a creative closure technique where we start by braiding a loop and finish with a button and tassel. The pretty button makes a great focal point and the tassel adds subtle movement. Also, when you choose a glass button, this bracelet is completely metal-free, making it ideal for those with metal allergies.

➤ Supplies
Kumihimo Toolkit
- standard thickness disk
- **8** weighted bobbins
- plain bobbin
- 90g center weight
- hemostat (optional)
- bead stopper
- tweezers (optional)

Other Materials
- size 18 nylon string:
  - 8 yd. color A
  - 4 yd. color B
  - 4 yd. color C
- 6–8g 6º Japanese seed beads
- ⅞" diameter button with shank
- 8–16 assorted small beads
- Hypo Cement

Finished Bracelet Length:
7½" (fits 6¼" wrist)

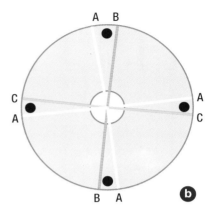

Set Up

Cut eight 2-yd. pieces of string (four color A, two color B, and two color C). Tie all eight pieces together using a loose overhand knot, positioning the knot 1 yd. from the end. Starting at one end of this knotted bundle, wind all the cords onto one plain bobbin, stopping just before the knot **(a)**.

Hold the bobbin below the hole in the kumihimo disk and pull the loose cords through. Position the loose cords in the standard eight-warp starting position (see p. 17), matching the color placement to the starting diagram **(b)**.

Wind each cord onto a weighted bobbin and attach the gator weight just below the knot **(c)**.

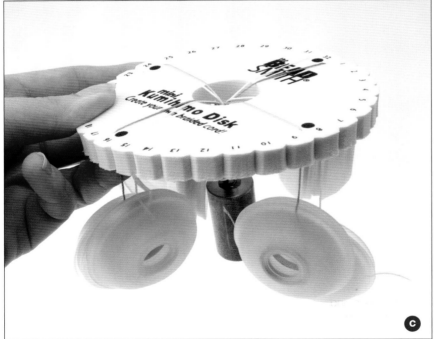

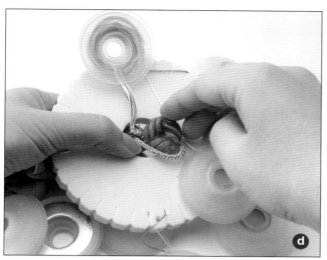

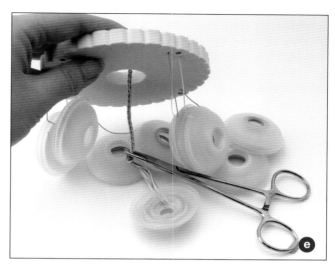

In this bracelet, I needed about 2¾" of braid to loop around the ⅞" button.

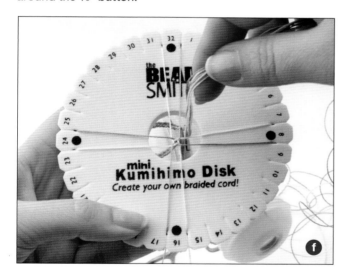

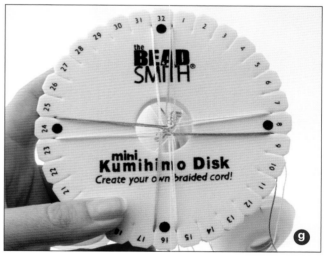

Making the Loop

Braid normally using the moves for a basketweave braid. Continue braiding until the length of the braid is long enough to make a loop around your button. You can check this by folding the braid and testing whether the button will fit through **(d)**.

Remove the gator weight and clip a hemostat clamp to the beginning of the braid just above the knot (if you don't have a hemostat, use the gator weight as a clamp) **(e)**. This will keep the braid from unraveling as you work. Remove the bobbin from the cords below the disk and carefully untie the knot. Pull the loose cords up through the hole in the disk **(f)**.

Matching up the colors, position one loose cord in each slot currently occupied. Now there are two cords per warp **(g)**. Try to keep the cords as tidy as possible with minimal crisscrossing. Remove the hemostat clamp.

Stringing the Beads

Remove the bobbin from one of the B or C warps. Rewind the bobbin using both strings in that position. Those two strings are now considered one warp. Do this for the other three B and C warps. These warps will not carry beads.

Remove the bobbin from one of the color A warps. Thread a big-eye needle onto one of the two strings that make up that warp and string 22 seed beads (tip, next page). Clip a bead stopper onto the string below the beads (the end of the beads farthest from the disk) and transfer the needle to the second string of that warp **(h)**. Sew through the beads a second time using the second string **(i)**.

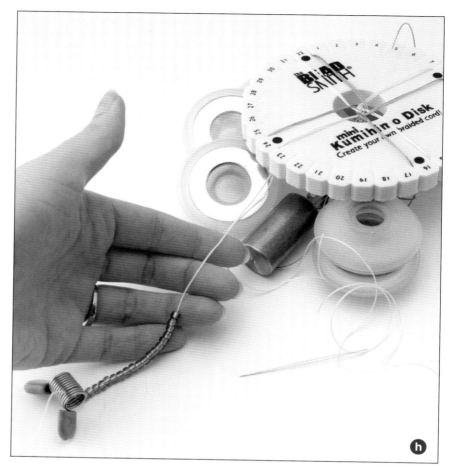

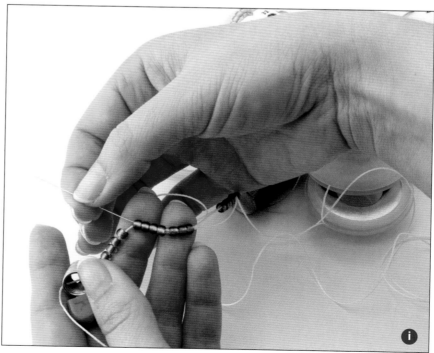

We're stringing the beads this way because there's too much bulk to fit through the bead hole if we tried using both strings at the same time. After you've strung both strings through the beads, tie the two ends together so the beads don't fall off.

The two strings are not exactly the same length. It's fine, but if it bothers you, feel free to trim the longer one so they match. Push the beads together as a group towards the disk so that they are about 2" below it. It is important to keep the beads together as a group so they don't get tangled with the string. Starting at the loose end, wind the two strings and beads onto the bobbin. Do this for the other three color A warps.

TIP

22 seed beads will make the bracelet 7½" long. A bracelet 7½" long will fit a 6¼" wrist. See sizing chart for other sizes.

Finished length measured from button shank to end of loop	Number of beads per warp	Bracelet fits wrist up to this size
7 1/2"	22	6 1/4"
8 1/8"	25	7"
9 1/4"	30	8"
This chart assumes a 7/8" button. Finished lengths may vary slightly with personal tension.		

My beads aren't sitting right. It looks like they're too close together.

A bead either didn't get placed correctly or popped out of place during the "without beads" sequence. Braid backwards (unbraid) until you come to the mistake. Be sure to fish the beads out of the braid while unbraiding. When you've unbraided back to the mistake, you can see there are two beads in one section. You need to un-braid this sequence completely and redo it so there is only one bead per section.

See how there are two beads in the south section? The one on the right should be in the east section.

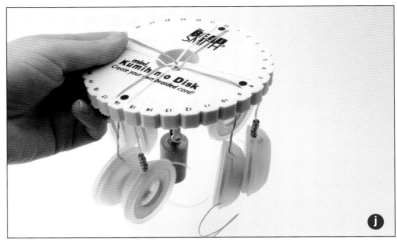

Braiding with Beads

Reposition the gator weight so it's clipped to the center of the loop. Braid two complete sequences without beads to get the newly-added warp strings at the correct point of braiding **(j)**. From here on out, you'll add beads every other sequence. Note that beads will only be added during the clockwise round of each sequence.

To add a bead, lift off the warp that needs to move and slide one bead forward. Allow the bead to fall to the point of braiding. Finish moving the warp, but don't let the bead jump over the neighboring warp **(k)**.

Do this for all four clockwise moves this round **(l)**.

Notice how there is only one bead in each section: north, south, east, and west. That's what you want. Also notice how each bead is in the same section as where it started. So the bead sitting in the north section was on the warp in the north positon before it moved. (That warp is now in the east position.)

Now finish the braiding sequence with counter-clockwise moves. There are no beads on these warps. These warps hug around the beads without sitting on top of them **(m)**.

Reset the disk and braid another complete sequence (clockwise and counter-clockwise), but don't add any beads **(n)**.

It's the round without beads that locks the beads in place and keeps them from moving. Continue adding beads in this way until you have reached your desired length. Remember that beads will be added every other sequence and only on clockwise moves.

I can't remember what I did last. Is it time to add beads or not?

Compare your work to the photos. Keep an eye on the point of braiding while you work. The more you do this, the easier it is to recognize what the braid looks like when it's time to add beads (or not).

This is what it looks like after adding beads. Now do a sequence without beads.

This is what it looks like after a sequence without beads. Now it is time to add beads.

33

Creative Closure: Button and Tassel

Braid without beads a length equal to half the width of your button. This will give you enough room to maneuver the button into the loop as you're putting on the bracelet. (For the sample bracelet, I braided ½" without beads.) Take the bobbin off warp 32 and cut off the knot at the end of the cords. Slide on a button and drop it into the braid as though it were a bead **(o, p)**.

You may need to give the button a shove to get it through the hole in the disk. Replace the bobbin you removed. Continue braiding until the unbeaded braid length is the same on both sides of the button. Remove all the bobbins. Holding the braid firmly below the disk at the point of braiding, remove the braid from the disk and tie an overhand knot as close as possible to the end of the braid. Glue the inside of the overhand knot using Hypo-Cement. Use the needle applicator to get in between the layers of the knot. Try not to get any glue on the outside of this knot **(q)**. Trim any knots at the ends of the warps.

Now we have 16 strings to play with for the tassel. Using an assortment of left-over seed beads from the bracelet and other color-coordinated beads from your stash, decorate the tassel by putting a bead on each string and tying a small knot about 1" from the large overhand knot at the end of the braid **(r)**.

You can make the tassel as long or short as you like. I like to make mine so each string is a different length. When using the 6º seed beads, put two strings through one bead so the knot will be large enough to stop the bead from falling off. Once you're satisfied with the beads and length of the tassel, trim the excess cording on the tassel. Glue each knot with a small dab of Hypo Cement. Give the glue a few minutes to dry.

TROUBLESHOOTING

My beads were locking just fine at the beginning of the bracelet, but now they keep popping out.

Make sure that your bracelet and the center weight aren't resting on anything (the table, your lap, etc.) while you braid. If the weight isn't dangling, it isn't helping. In fact if your braid is resting on the table, it may even be pushing up above the surface of the disk. That disrupts the tension you're trying to maintain and can lead to "escapee" beads.

I'm out of beads, but my braid isn't long enough.

No problem. If you're out of beads, but you'd like to keep going, just unwind the bobbin, cut off or untie the knot, and string more beads.

Did one warp run out of beads before the others? What happened? Look at your braid. The beads should be sitting in neat little clusters of four beads. If a cluster is missing a bead, then you forgot to add a bead to that position. If all the clusters have exactly four beads, then you miscounted while stringing.

There doesn't seem to be any place for my beads to go.

Is the point of braiding centered in the hole? If not, there won't be enough space between the point of braiding and the foam disk. Tug gently on the warps to move the point of braiding back closer to center. Try to keep your tension even as you braid so the point of braiding stays centered.

Rodeo Queen
Bracelet

Creative Closure

The trouble with bracelets is getting the size just right. There's a lot of wiggle room in a necklace, but a bracelet that is too big or too small just won't work. This project solves that problem by incorporating an *adjustable sliding closure*. The closure works on friction so keep that in mind when choosing your core material. It can't be too slippery. Satin rattail, for example, wouldn't work very well because it would keep pulling through the seed bead and the bracelet would open up. I chose Chinese knotting cord because it has some tooth to it, and the two pieces grip each other inside the bead.

The Chinese knotting cord is a core, not one of the warps. That means that we'll be braiding around it and it won't get a slot on the disk. This core trick is pretty neat and means you can add an adjustable slide closure to any basketweave braid, even if your main braiding material is too slippery.

➤ **Supplies**

Kumihimo Toolkit
- standard thickness disk
- **8** plain bobbins
- 90g center weight
- tweezers or a toothpick (optional)
- thread zapper (optional)

Other Materials
- **4** 30" pieces of suede leather, ⅛"-wide strips (**1** each of **4** colors)
- 18" 1.5mm Chinese knotting cord
- **2** cones with 6–7mm inside diameter at widest point
- **3** 3º Japanese seed beads

Finished Bracelet Length: adjustable to fit 6½"–8¼" wrist

Note: Make sure that a piece of Chinese knotting cord can fit through the cone.

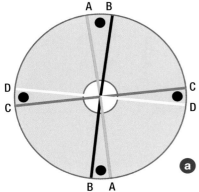

Set Up

Find the middle point of a 30" piece of suede. Holding the middle point centered over the hole in the kumihimo disk, lock the suede in place following the starting diagram **(a, b)**.

Do this for each 30" piece of suede. Wind each warp onto a bobbin.

Cut an 18" piece of Chinese knotting cord. Feed the knotting cord between the intersecting pieces of suede at the point of braiding **(c)**.

Position the knotting cord so 6" is hanging below the disk. Tie the suede together at the point of braiding using a scrap piece of thread **(d)**.

Clip the center weight to the suede below the disk. Don't clip the weight to the knotting cord or it will pull through.

Braiding

We're going to braid around the knotting cord. It doesn't get a slot in the disk. It just sits on top and we'll keep moving it out of the way as we work. I like to keep the core in the top-left quadrant while I do the first three clockwise moves **(e)**. Then I move the core to the top-right quadrant while I do the last clockwise move and the first three counter-clockwise moves **(f)**.

Then I move the core back to the top-left quadrant to finish the counter-clockwise moves. Then I reposition the warps and begin the sequence again. It doesn't matter where the core hangs out while you braid, so long as you don't braid over it.

Creative Closure: Adjustable Sliding Clasp

When your braid is 6½" long, remove it from the disk and tie the suede leather and knotting cord in a temporary overhand knot. Relax the braid and then tightly bind it. Untie the overhand knot. Carefully snip the excess suede very close to the binding, but do not cut the Chinese knotting cord core **(g)**. We'll need the core to make the clasp.

Snip any tails from the binding thread or the scrap thread used to tie the suede together during the set up. Feed one end of the knotting cord through a cone and glue in place using E6000 **(h)**.

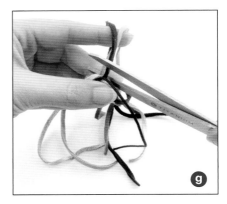

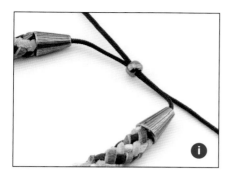

Repeat for the other end of the bracelet and allow to dry for 24 hours.

Feed both pieces of knotting cord through the 3º seed bead in opposite directions. It's an extremely tight fit (just what you're looking for in a friction clasp), so you may need sharp tweezers or a toothpick to poke the cords through. Pull the cords in opposite directions to close the bracelet. This is the smallest size. Now open the bracelet back up as much as necessary to fit over the widest part of your hand **(i)**.

Take note of how much core is showing on either side of the bead. Don't tie the finishing knots any shorter than this from the clasp bead. On my bracelet, it's 1¼" with the bracelet in this open position. Slide a 3º seed bead onto each piece of knotting cord and tie an overhand knot to finish. Trim the excess cord. Secure the knots with glue or melt the ends with a thread zapper.

No-Knot Start

I usually start my projects by determining how long my warps should be (based on the 3-to-1 rule) and then cutting however many cords I need for a project (8 or 16). Tying the warps together is an easy way to set up a braid, but now I'm going to teach you a way to save on wasted fiber. I call it the "No-Knot Start."

We'll cut half as many warp pieces, but they'll be twice as long. Then we'll start braiding from the middle. For example, "Double-Take Necklace" (p. 16) called for 12 yd. of satin cord cut into eight 1½-yd. pieces. For a no-knot start, we would still use the same 12 yd. of satin cord, but instead, cut it into four 3-yd. pieces.

Once we've cut the double-length warps, there are two ways to get them onto the disk.

Option 1: Find the middle point of one of the warps. Holding the middle of the cord centered over the hole in the kumihimo disk, lock it in place. Do this for each of the warps. Bind the warps

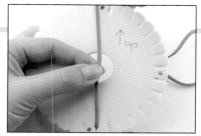

together at the point of braiding using binding thread. We used this option in the "Rodeo Queen Bracelet" because it let us sneak a core into the braid.

Option 2: Line up the ends of all the warps. Fold in half to find the middle. Tie the warps together at the middle using beading thread or some scrap string.
Holding the tied, middle point over the hole in the kumihimo disk, lock in the cords in place in the standard starting position for your braid. Wind each warp onto a bobbin and braid as usual.

Note: This neat trick can only work for the start of the braid.

The advantages:
• A no-knot start saves several inches of waste.
• Sometimes you don't have as much fiber as you want or it comes in a pre-cut length. You can maximize your finished braid with a no-knot start.

Braiding with Suede

Suede has a fuzzy side and a smooth side. If you want, you can pay extra attention while braiding and try to keep the suede from flipping around while you work. Sometimes I paid attention and sometimes I let the suede twist from fuzzy side out to smooth side out. If you have a fuzzy or smooth preference for your braid, whichever side of the suede is facing up (fuzzy or smooth) will face the inside of the braid and will less visible in the finished project. Don't ruin your good kumihimo scissors by cutting the suede. Use your general crafting scissors for this project.

Pirouette
Necklace

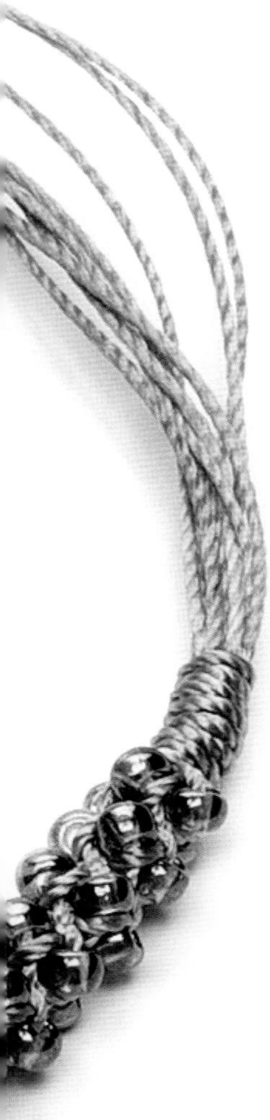

Finally, those of us in the kumihimo club get to use the new two-hole beads in a meaningful way. Sure, you could just ignore that second hole and braid away—but where's the fun in that? In this lovely necklace, the second hole of the two-hole lentils is integral to the design. It's what allows you to stitch the focal piece into a graceful twist.

Creative Closure

➤ Supplies

Kumihimo Toolkit
- standard thickness disk
- **8** weighted bobbins
- plain bobbin
- 45g or 90g center weight
- big-eye needle

Other Materials
- 16 yd. size 18 nylon braiding string
- 6" piece of satin cord (this is used as a tool)
- 5g 8° Japanese seed beads
- 1g 11° Japanese seed beads
- **48** two-hole lentil beads
- beading thread to match lentils
- Hypo Cement
- **2** 6mm soldered jump rings
- clasp
- **2** 6mm jump rings

Finished Necklace Length: 19½"

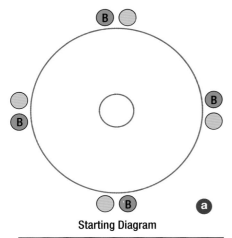

Starting Diagram

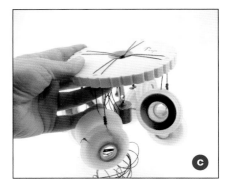

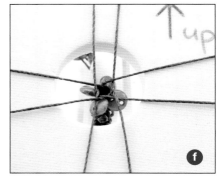

Set Up

Cut eight 2-yd. pieces of string. Find the middle of the strings and tie all eight together using a loose overhand knot. Put the knot through the hole in the disk so you have eight strings below the disk and eight strings above. Arrange the strings on top of the disk in the standard starting position. (Refer to the starting diagram if using two colors **(a)**.)

Following the starting diagram, string the following set of beads on only the four "B" warps: nine 8º seed beads, 12 two-hole lentils (string through one hole only), and nine 8º seed beads **(b)**.

Tie a knot on the end of the warp so the beads don't fall off. Starting with the knotted end, wind each warp onto a weighted bobbin. Wind each of the four plain warps (no beads) onto a weighted bobbin. Clip the center weight to the knot below the disk **(c)**.

Wind the eight strings below the disk onto the plain bobbin.

Braiding

Braid four complete sequences of basketweave kumihimo without adding any beads. From here on out, you'll add beads every other sequence. Note that beads will only be added during the clockwise round of each sequence.

To add a bead, lift off the warp that needs to move and slide one bead forward. Allow the bead to fall to the point of braiding. Finish moving the warp. Do this for all four clockwise moves this round. The bead will get locked into place by the counter-clockwise round of the sequence. Reset the disk and braid another complete sequence (clockwise and counter-clockwise), but don't add any beads. Continue adding beads in this way until you have added the first nine seed beads from each warp. Remember that beads will be added every other sequence and only on clockwise moves.

The lentil beads are added in the same way. While making a clockwise move, lift the warp, slide one bead forward and allow it to fall to the point of braiding. Finish moving the warp. Do this for all four clockwise moves this round **(d)**.

The counter-clockwise sequence will begin to push the beads down, but won't fully lock them into place because of their size **(e)**.

Don't worry! Just keep braiding. The first clockwise round of the next sequence (remember this time it is without adding beads) will lock the lentils into place **(f)**.

I find it helpful to tug ever-so-slightly upward on each warp as I move it during this round without beads. This way, the beads get pushed below the working warps and can't get caught in the middle of the braid. After adding all of the lentils on each warp, continue adding beads every other sequence until you have used all of the seed beads.

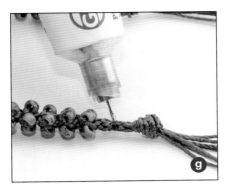

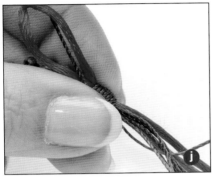

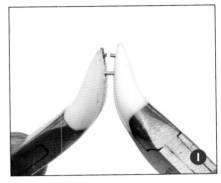

Creative Closure: Finishing the Braid

After adding the last round of seed beads, braid four complete sequences of basketweave (clockwise and counter-clockwise) without adding any beads. Remove the bobbins and the center weight. With one hand, pinch the braid at the point of braiding immediately below the disk. With the other hand, remove the warps from their slots and set the disk aside. Tie the warps together using a loose overhand knot. Use beading thread to bind the braid right next to the knot. Closely trim the tails of the binding thread. Untie the loose overhand knot. Glue the binding with Hypo-Cement **(g)**.

Cover all sides of the binding with the glue. Do the same at the other end of the braid. Let dry 5–10 minutes.

Making a Decorative Knot

The eight cords dangling from either side of the braid will become the sides of the necklace. On one side of the necklace, identify the longest cord and trim the knot from the end (if it has one), but leave the cord as long as possible.

This cord will be used for the decorative knot.

The 6" piece of satin is your knotting tool. Fold it in half. Set the knotting tool on top of the beaded braid with the folded end towards the beads **(h)**.

The knotting tool is parallel to your braid. Holding the knotting tool in place with one hand, use your other hand to wrap the longest cord (the one you trimmed) around the bound braid and the knotting tool. Wrap towards the beaded braid **(i)**.

Think Goldilocks when wrapping—not too tight, not too lose. Make as many wraps as needed to reach the beads. When your last wrap is as close to the beads as possible without going over them, bring the wrapping cord through the knotting tool. Holding the wraps in one hand, use your other hand to pull the tails of the knotting tool **(j)**.

This will pull the wrapping cord under the wraps. It may take some tugging to accomplish this. If it really won't go, you've wrapped too tightly. Unwrap and try again. Put a dab of glue inside the decorative knot by working the

needle tip of the Hypo-Cement under the wraps. Make a decorative knot on the other side of the necklace.

Adding the Clasp and Tassels

Cut an 18" piece of beading thread. On one side of the necklace, pass all eight cords through a soldered jump ring 6½" from the decorative knot. Fold the warps over the ring and bind in place **(k)**.

Glue the binding and let dry 10 minutes. Use the longest cord to make a decorative knot. Repeat on the other side of the necklace.

Use a jump ring to attach one half of a clasp to each soldered jump ring. Cut the tassel to the desired length. String one seed bead on the end of each tassel cord and tie a small knot. Glue each knot with a dab of Hypo Cement.

TIP

Remember that when opening and closing jump rings, you hold one side of the ring still and push the other side away from or towards you. Never pull the rings straight out to the side **(l)**.

Embellishing

There are four rows of lentils. Each will be embellished separately.

While embellishing, you will only be using the second holes of the lentils (the free holes), not the ones that were used to add the lentils to the braid. When I say to go through the lentil, that's what I mean.

Rows 1 and 2

Cut a 36" piece of beading thread. Thread a needle on one end. Sew through the last lentil in a row, leaving a 6" tail. Anchor the thread by sewing through the same hole two more times (the thread will show) **(m)**.

Pick up an 11º seed bead and sew through the next lentil **(n)**.

Continue the pattern of picking up an 11º and sewing through the next lentil until you reach the end of the row **(o)**.

Pull the thread tightly enough so it pulls the lentils into a lovely curved shape. Anchor the thread at the end of the row by sewing through the last lentil several times. Sew back into the row of beads and finish off the thread by tying a couple of half-hitch knots. To make a half-hitch knot, you sew under the thread between two beads

and then sew through the loop that forms **(p, q)**.

Sew through 2–4 more beads and then trim the thread close. Transfer the needle to the 6" tail at the start of the row and finish in the same way. Repeat this embellishment on one of the adjacent rows of lentils **(r)**.

Rows 3 and 4

Cut a 36" piece of beading thread. Thread a needle on one end. Sew through the last lentil in a row leaving a 6" tail. Anchor the thread by sewing through the same hole two more times. The thread will show. Pick up an 11º, an 8º, and an 11º. Sew through the next lentil **(s)**.

Continue the pattern of picking up an 11º, an 8º, and an 11º and sewing through the next lentil until you reach the

end of the row. Pull the thread tight so it pulls the lentils into a curve. Anchor thread at the end of the row by sewing through the last lentil several times. The thread will show. Sew back into the row of beads and finish off the thread by tying a couple of half-hitch knot. Sew through the next 2–4 beads and then trim the thread close. Transfer the needle to the 6" tail at the start of the row and finish in the same way. Repeat this embellishment on the last row of lentils.

Eight-Warp Half-Round
BRAID

Kara Yatsu

Most people think of round braids when they think of kumihimo, but it comes in other shapes as well. This braid structure is flat on one side and domed on the other, so it's a "half-round" braid. It's possible to incorporate beads into a half-round braid. As you'll see with "Harmony" and "Mythic Adventure," the beads sit neatly along one edge.

This braid is called *Kara Yatsu* in Japanese. *Kara* means from China and *Yatsu* means eight so we can understand this name as an eight-warp braid from China.

Charm *Bracelet*

The half-round braid is a bit more complicated than the basketweave, so go slowly as you're learning and be patient with yourself. Once you get the hang of it, you'll be rewarded with a braid that's full of possibilities! I embellished my braid with metal charms, but you could also try wire-wrapping some small beads and adding them as dangles.

➤ Supply List

Kumihimo Toolkit
- **8** plain bobbins
- 45g center weight

Other Materials
- 16' 1mm satin cord
  - 8' color A
  - 4' color B
  - 4' color C
- **2** 5–6mm inside diameter cones
- **2** 8° seed beads (optional)
- clasp
- **2** 4–6mm jump rings
- **10** 6mm ID hammered rings
- assorted charms and 4–6mm jump rings to attach them

Finished Bracelet Length:
8¼" (fits 7" wrist)

Set Up

Cut eight 24" pieces of satin rattail (four color A, two color B, and two color C). Tie all eight pieces together at one end using an overhand knot. Lock the warps in place on the disk following the starting diagram **(a)**. Wind each warp onto a bobbin. Attach the center weight below the knot.

Braiding

Using your right hand, lift the top-left warp out of its slot and cross diagonally to the right. Place it in the slot just below the pair of warps on the right side of the disk **(b)**.

Using your left hand, lift the top-right warp out of its slot and cross diagonally to the left. Place it in the slot just below the pair of warps on the left side of the disk **(c)**.

Now you have three warps on the left, three warps on the right, two at the bottom, and none on top. It's normal for your point of braiding to shift a bit towards the bottom of the hole at this point because of the uneven distribution of warps.

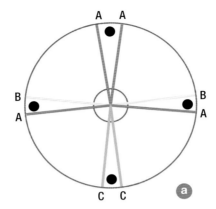

32 → 10

1 → 23

17 → 7

16 → 26

8 → 16

Using your right hand, lift the bottom-left warp out of its slot and cross diagonally to the right. Place it in the slot just above the three warps on the right side of the disk **(d)**.

Using your left hand, lift the bottom-right warp out of its slot and cross diagonally to the left. Place it in the slot just above the three warps on the left side of the disk **(e)**.

Now you have four warps on the left and four warps on the right. This layout makes me think of cat whiskers and is an easily recognizable mid-sequence stopping point. Looking at the cat whiskers, notice only four of the warps

are adjacent to a dot. These are the warps that haven't moved yet this sequence. These are the warps you'll be working with for the next four moves. For the first four moves of this braid, warps were crossing from left to right or from right to left. For the last four moves of this braid, warps don't change sides. If it starts on the right, it stays on the right. If it starts on the left, it stays on the left.

Using your right hand, lift the warp just above the right dot out of its slot. Place it in the slot to the right of the bottom dot **(f)**.

How can I unbraid?

If you discover a mistake in your braid, as always, your options are to ignore it or fix it. If you want to fix a mistake, the first step is backing up the braid until you reach the mistake. To unbraid, carefully do the braiding sequence in reverse. Remember that since the last step of the braiding sequence is to close the side gaps, the first step of unbraiding is to make side gaps. You do that by moving each warp on the left and right sides one slot away from the dots.

As you braid, pay attention to how the warps look at the point of braiding. By paying close attention, you can spot mistakes right away and you won't have to undo a lot of work to fix them. Here are two of the most common braiding errors.

Accidentally crossing the warps at either the top or bottom position

Warps only cross sides during the first half of the sequence in the half-round braid. After the "cat whiskers" position, warps should stay on the side they start on.

These bottom warps should be parallel.

25 → 17

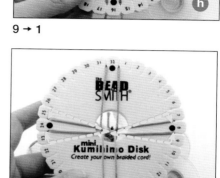

9 → 1

24 → 32

26 → 25, 23 → 24, 7 → 8, 10 → 9

Using your left hand, lift the warp just above the left dot out of its slot. Place it in the slot to the left of the bottom dot **(g)**.

Using your right hand, lift the warp just below the right dot out of its slot. Place it in the slot to the right of the top dot **(h)**.

Using your left hand, lift the warp just below the left dot out of its slot. Place it in the slot to the left of the top dot **(i)**. Well done! That's the end of the sequence. Now you have two warps at the top, two at the bottom, two on the left, and two on the right. On the left and right sides, there are two empty slots between the warps. Before beginning the next sequence, close those gaps by moving each of the left and right warps one slot closer to the dots **(j)**.

Braid until one warp is too short to continue, and then remove the braid from the disk and knot the end.

TIPS FOR LEARNING THE BRAID
- Each warp moves only once per sequence.
- Complete the eight-move sequence and then reset everything back to the starting positon before beginning the sequence again.
- Alternate hands while braiding. Use the hand of the warp's destination. For example, in the first move the top-left warp moves to a position on the right side of the disk. I use my right hand because the movement finishes on the right.

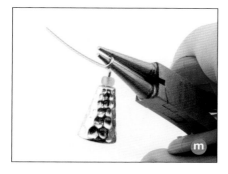

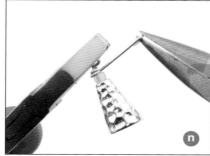

Failing to cross sides during the first half of the sequence

There is a hole in the braid.

Remember that the first two pairs of moves in this braid call for the warps to cross sides. If they don't cross, you'll get a hole in the center of the braid. Unbraid to the error and correct it.

Incorrect. The light pink warps should be crossed.

Wire-Wrapping the Cones

String a headpin up through the cone wide-end first. String an 8º seed bead on the headpin to coordinate with the braid, if you like. With the tip of your chainnose pliers, grasp the wire directly above the cone. Bend the wire (above the pliers) into a right angle (k). Position the jaws of your roundnose pliers in the bend and bring the wire over the top jaw (l). Reposition the pliers' lower jaw snugly into the loop. Curve the wire around the bottom of the roundnose pliers (m).

Position the flatnose pliers' jaws across the loop and wrap the wire around the wire stem, covering the stem between the loop and the cone (n).

Trim the excess wire and press the cut end close to the wraps with chainnose pliers. Now this cone is an endcap! Repeat for the second cone.

Assembly

Relax the braid and then bind and cut it to your desired length. Slide 10 hammered rings onto the braid. I attached my charms to the second, fifth, and ninth hammered rings using jump rings. Space your charms as you like, depending on the number of charms in your collection. Glue on the endcaps and allow to dry 24 hours. Use jump rings to attach a toggle clasp half to each end of the bracelet.

Leather Wrap
Bracelet

One of the things I find most fascinating with kumihimo is how dramatically you can change the look of a braid by changing the material. When done with leather, the half-round braid spreads out and becomes almost flat. The negative space adds to the texture and gives the bracelet an organic feel.

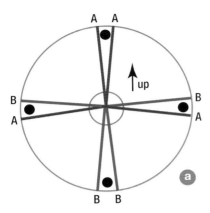

> ### Supplies
> *Kumihimo Toolkit*
> - standard thickness disk
> - **8** plain bobbins
> - 90g center weight
> - craft scissors

Other Materials
- 1.5mm round leather cord
  - 8' color A
  - 8' color B
- 8mm endcaps or cones
- toggle clasp
- **2–6** 4mm jump rings

Finished Bracelet Length:
approx. 18" including the clasp
(wraps around twice)

Set Up

To conserve leather, you'll use a "no-knot start" similar to the "Rodeo Queen Bracelet," p. 35. This time, though, you'll bind the warps together before putting them on the disk. Cut four 48" pieces of leather using craft scissors. Bind them together at the middle. Hold the binding over the hole in the kumihimo disk and lock each warp in place following the starting diagram **(a)**.

Clip the gator weight to the leather at the point of braiding **(b)**.

Braiding

Braid using the half-round sequence (see p. 45) until one warp is too short to lock in place, and then remove the braid from the disk. Tightly bind the loose end of the braid. Cut off the excess leather using craft scissors, and then glue an endcap to each end of the braid. Allow to dry for 24 hours and then attach the clasp using jump rings. The bracelet wraps around your wrist twice.

NOTE

I like to use an 8mm endcap for this project because I don't like to need to work hard to fit the endcap on. Some of my students prefer a tighter fit. They bind the braid as tightly as possible and squeeze it into a 6mm endcap.

Harmony
Necklace

➤ **Supply List**

Kumihimo Toolkit
- standard thickness disk
- 8 plain bobbins
- 45g center weight

Other Materials
- 12 yd. 2mm hand-dyed satin cord
- **50** teardrop beads (Unicorne)
- 6mm magnetic endcaps
- Optional: white craft glue

Finished Necklace Length: approx. 21"

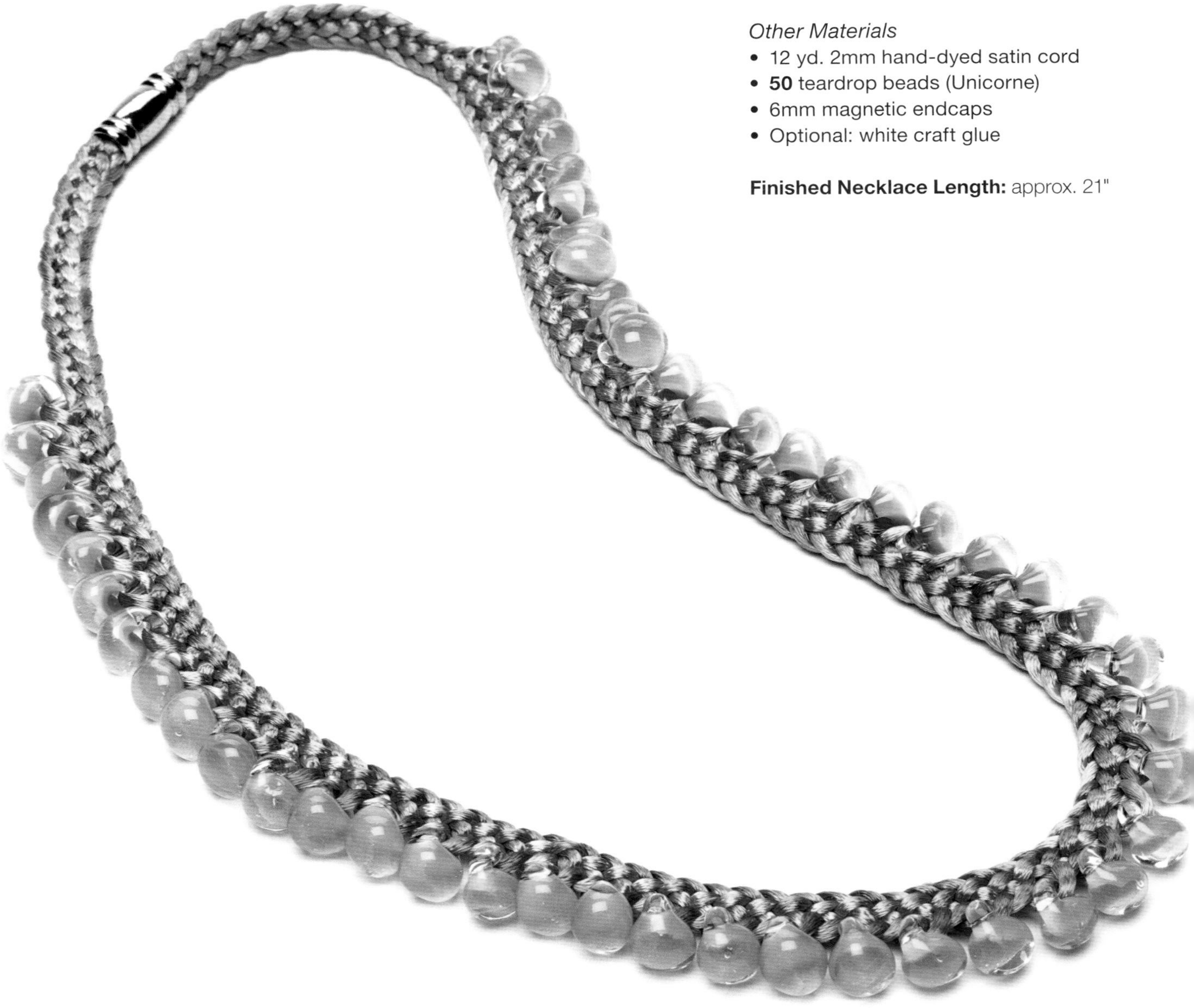

Often times with kumihimo, you have to choose what will take center stage: the beads or the braid? In this necklace, they work together. The teardrop beads hang gracefully from the edge of the braid; their size and shape complement the texture of the braid and enhance it.

The teardrop beads used in this piece are from an American company called Unicorne. I chose them for this project, not just because of their beautiful shape, but for their large hole size. There are also a variety of Czech teardrop and mushroom beads with similar shapes, but the holes are way too tiny to accommodate the satin cord.

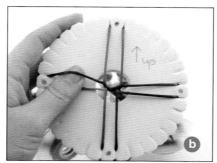

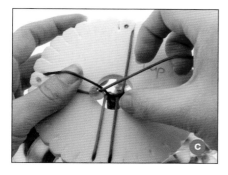

Set Up

Cut eight 54" pieces of satin cord. Tie them together using an overhand knot. Lock in place on the disk using the standard starting position for an eight-warp braid (see p. 45). Wind each warp onto a bobbin. Attach a gator weight below the knot and begin braiding using the half-round braiding sequence. Braid 3". On each of the top two warps (position 32 and 1), remove the bobbin, string 25 teardrop beads, and rewind the warp onto a bobbin.

TIP

If you are having trouble stringing the beads onto the satin cord, try stiffening the end of the satin with a bit of craft glue. Only a few of the teardrop beads will fit inside the bobbin, so most will sit between the disk and the bobbin **(a).**

From here on out, every time you do the first move in the sequence (32–>10), slide one bead into the center of the braid and lock it under the upper west warp (25). This can be a bit awkward, so watch how I do it. First, I use my left thumb to raise the upper west warp (25) **(b)**. Then I use my right hand to lift the top-left warp out of its slot and let one bead slide down to the point of braiding. I use my right thumb to nudge the

bead into position under the raised upper west warp **(c)**, making sure the bulbous part of the teardrop bead is pointing down and away from the point of braiding. I take my left thumb out from under the upper west warp and my right hand completes the move by crossing diagonally to the right **(d)**.

That's it for adding beads this sequence. You only add one bead per sequence, and you do it on the first move. Don't move a bead when the top-right warp crosses diagonally to the left (1–>23). Ignore the beads if they are in any position other than the top-left (32). All other moves are completed as usual without any changes. There will be a bead in the top-left position every other sequence. Once you have braided in all the beads, continue braiding without beads until you run out of cord. Remove the braid from the disk and tie an overhand knot. Give the braid a good end-to-end stretch to relax the braid and help the beads sit neatly. Bind each end of the braid 2½" from the beads. Make sure the bindings are even and then cut off the excess braid and glue on endcaps. Let dry for 24 hours.

(see p. 45)

TROUBLESHOOTING

Check your work every inch or so to make sure all of the beads are lying on the same side of the braid, all beads are locked in place correctly, and you haven't missed any beads.

There's a missing bead!

Oops! It's easy to get into a zone and forget to add a bead since you're not doing it every move. Carefully unbraid back to the empty spot and correct your work.

Beads on both sides: The trick to getting the beads to line up nicely all on one side of the braid is to only add a bead when doing the first move of the sequence. If you add beads on both the first and second moves of the sequence, they'll lie on both sides of the braid. Carefully unbraid back to the extra bead and remove it.

Kumihimo Math

Want to make the necklace longer? No problem! The easiest way to add length is to lengthen the plain braid sections at either end of the necklace.

The 50 teardrop beads make a beaded section 16" long. Take your desired length and subtract 16" for the beaded section and then subtract the length added by your endcap and clasp. (Most magnetic endcaps add less than ¼".) This tells you how long the plain braid portion of your necklace needs to be. Divide that number by two so you know how much plain braid is needed for each side of the necklace.

Let's try it together with some real numbers:
I want to make a 24" necklace and this time I'm going to use some cones and a toggle that are 1" long when assembled. I take my 24" desired finished length and subtract 16" for the beaded section. Now I have 8". Take the 8" and subtract 1" for the clasp. Now I have 7". That means that 7" of my 24" necklace will be plain braid. I want that length evenly divided with half on each side of the necklace, so I divide 7" by 2 and get

3½". I need 3½" of plain braid at the start and finish of my necklace.

Keep in mind the maximum length from 12 yd. of 2mm satin cord is typically 24". If you want a necklace longer than that, you'll need more satin. Use the three-to-one rule to calculate how long to cut each warp.

Want a shorter necklace?
Ok, we can do that, too! With precious beads like the teardrops, it's best not to waste them in the back where they won't be seen. So if we're going shorter, we'll probably want to use fewer beads. Take your desired finished length and subtract the length of your clasp. Then subtract the length of your plain braid sections. This tells you how long your beaded section will be. Multiply the length of your beaded section by 3.2 beads* to calculate how many total beads you need for your necklace. Divide by two to know how many beads to string on each of the two north warps.

⅛"
magnetic
endcap

2½"
unbeaded section

16"
beaded section

Again, this is clearer when we work through it with real numbers. Let's make a 16" necklace with magnetic endcaps. I'll start with my desired finished length of 16" and subtract ¼" for the tiny amount added by the magnetic endcap and I get 15¾". From that, I subtract 5" for my plain braid sections (2½" on each side) and get 10¾". This is how long my beaded section needs to be. Multiply 10.75 by 3.2 (get out the calculator) and you get 34.4 beads. Round that up to 35 and that's the total number of beads you need for the necklace. It doesn't divide evenly by two, so we'll string 18 on the top-left warp and 17 on the top-right warp.

The teardrops work up about 3.2 beads per braided inch in this pattern. How do I know? I measured my sample necklaces.

TROUBLESHOOTING

Bead in the middle of the braid: If the bead doesn't get locked in place under the upper west warp, it will be trapped in the middle of the braid. Thankfully, this boo-boo usually gets noticed pretty quickly. Just unbraid back to the trapped bead and position it correctly under the upper west warp.

2½"
beaded section

⅛"
magnetic
endcap

**Total Necklace Length: 21¼",
when clasped**

Mythic Adventure
Cuff

The texture of this cuff is amazing! The flat braids along the edge frame the interlocking beads down the middle. Run your fingers over the beads and they feel pebbly and smooth like snakeskin—or maybe dragon skin? Hmm... I enjoy a rich fantasy life, and to me this bracelet seems perfect to adorn the wrist of someone on a quest.

> ➤ **Supply List:**

Kumihimo Toolkit
- double-thick disk
- **8** plain bobbins
- 90g center weight
- big-eye needle
- #10 beading needle

Other Materials
- 12 yd. size 18 nylon string
- 3 yd. micro string
- 1–2g 11º seed beads
- 2–3g SuperDuo beads
- 1–2g Mini SuperDuo beads
- beading thread in two colors (one to match the seed beads and one to match the regular SuperDuos)
- **4** 3mm endcaps
- **4** 4mm jump rings
- **2** sets ball-and-socket clasps
- Hypo Cement

Finished Bracelet Length: approx. 7" (fits 6¾" wrist)

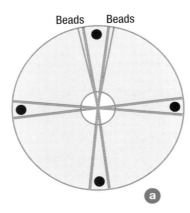

Beads   Beads

a

Set Up

For this braid, we'll use size 18 nylon string as our main fiber—one piece of it per warp. 11º seed beads don't string easily onto the size 18 cord, so we're going to use some micro string as a carrier thread. This means on every warp with beads (two warps in this case), there will be a piece of micro string in addition to the size 18 string. The two strings will run parallel to each other, share a slot, and be wound onto the same bobbin. The beads will just be threaded onto the micro string.

Cut eight 54" pieces of size 18 nylon string and two 54" pieces of micro nylon string, tie everything together using an overhand knot, and lock the strings on the kumihimo disk in the standard starting position (see p. 45). Each warp in the north position (32 and 1) will have a piece of micro string in addition to the size 18 string **(a)**.

Use a big-eye needle to string twenty 11º seed beads on each piece of micro string. Attach the center weight below the point of braiding.

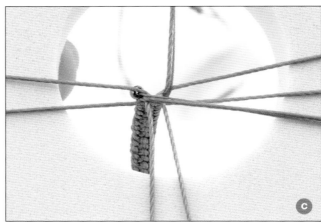

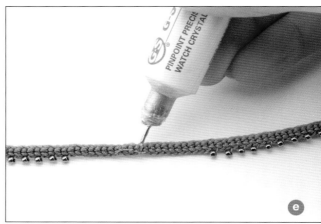

Braiding

Braid a half-inch section without beads. After you've completed the half-inch of plain braid, it's time to start incorporating the beads. Add beads as in the "Harmony Necklace," p. 50. Whenever there are beads on warp 32, add a bead to the braid as you complete the first move in the sequence: Lift the top-left warp out of its slot and slide one bead down to the point of braiding. Use your left thumb to raise warp 25 and use your right hand to nudge the bead just under warp 25 so it is locked in place between warps 25 and 24 **(b)**.

The top-left warp continues its move and locks in place below the warps on the right hand side **(c)**.

Continue the rest of the braid sequence as usual. You only add one bead per sequence and you do it on the first move. Don't move a bead when the top-right warp crosses down and to the left (1–>23). Ignore the beads if they are in any position other than the top-left (32). There will be a bead in the top-left position every other sequence.

TIP

Try to keep the two strings on each bead warp parallel as your work. If they twist together, it will be harder to slide a bead into place. When the main warp string and the micro carrier thread get twisted around each other, as with the bobbin on the right, it is difficult to slide the beads into place **(d)**.

Once you've braided in all of the beads, double-check your braid to make sure that there are 40 seed beads along the edge. There are. Excellent! Now we're going to braid the other half of the bracelet. We'll cut them apart later, but for now it will just be one long braid. Braid 1½" without beads. Now string 20 11º seed beads on each of the carrier threads like we did before. Remember your warps with carrier threads may be in positions 32 and 1 or 24 and 9, depending on where you left off in the braid. When your bead warps are in the north positions, resume adding beads as before. When you are out of beads, double-check your braid to make sure that this section also has 40 beads along the edge. It's important in this design for both sections to have the same number of beads. Braid a half-inch without beads. Remove the bobbins and the center weight. Remove the braid from the disk and tie the warps together using an overhand knot.

With the braid off the disk, we need to cut it in half so we have two separate braids. In the center of the unbeaded section, make two bindings ¼" apart. Put a dab of Hypo-Cement on each binding **(e)** and allow to dry for five minutes. Cut between the two bindings to divide the braid in two.

Adding SuperDuos

Count out 39 Super Duo beads. Use a needle to make sure both holes of every bead are open. Sometimes the coating clogs one of the holes and you'll be really frustrated if you discover it after adding the bead to the project.

Cut 24" of beading thread in a color that matches the 11º seed beads. Thread a #10 needle on one end and sew through the first seed bead at one end of the braid, leaving an 8" tail. It doesn't matter which end of the braid you start with, but being right-handed, I found it most comfortable to work from bottom to top with the seed beads on the right side of the braid **(f)**.

Sew through the same seed bead two more times to anchor the thread. Pick up a SuperDuo (sewing through only one hole) and sew through the next seed bead **(g)**.

Continue this pattern of picking up a Super Duo and sewing through the next seed bead. When you reach the last seed bead, sew through it two more times to secure and then sew back into the beads. Finish off the thread with a couple of half-hitch knots, spaced a few beads apart. Sew through 2–4 more beads. Transfer the needle to the 8" tail,

sew back into the beads, and finish off the thread by tying a couple of half-hitch knots. Sew through 2–4 more beads. Remove the needle and trim both thread tails.

Repeat this step for the other half of the bracelet.

Adding the Mini SuperDuos

Count out 38 Mini Super Duo beads. Use a needle to make sure both holes of every bead are open. Cut 24" of beading thread in the color that best matches the regular SuperDuos. Thread a needle on one end and sew through the empty hole of the first regular SuperDuo in the row, leaving an 8" tail. Anchor the thread by sewing through this same hole two more times. Pick up a Mini SuperDuo (sewing through only one hole), and sew through the empty hole of the next regular SuperDuo **(h)**.

Continue this pattern of picking up a Mini SuperDuo and sewing through the next Regular SuperDuo. When you reach the last regular Super Duo, sew through it two more times to secure and then sew back into the row of regular and Mini SuperDuos. Finish off the thread the same way you did when adding the regular SuperDuos.

Kumihimo Math

The beaded section with 20 beads per warp is 5½" long when finished. For every extra inch of length desired, string an additional four seed beads per warp.

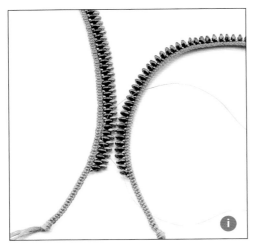

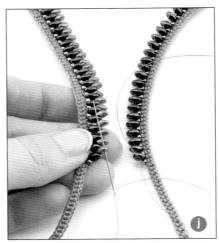

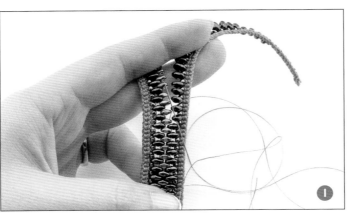

Zipping It Up

Now we're going to zip the two sides of the bracelet together by stitching the Mini SuperDuos on one braid to the regular SuperDuos on the other braid. Start by arranging your two braids so the braid with the Mini SuperDuos is on the left and the other braid is on the right. The cut ends of both braids are at the top **(i)**.

Next, we'll anchor thread to the first regular SuperDuo of the braid on the right. Cut 24" of beading thread in a color matching the regular SuperDuos. Thread a needle on one end and sew into the empty hole of the first regular SuperDuo. Sew through it two more times to secure. Sew through the empty hole of the first Mini SuperDuo on the left braid **(j)**.

Sew through the empty hole of the next regular SuperDuo on the right braid **(k)**.

Continue this pattern of sewing through a Mini SuperDuo on the left braid and then through a regular SuperDuo on the right braid. I find it helpful to hold the braids in my hand as I work, rather than letting everything sit on the table **(l)**.

When your thread is exiting the last regular SuperDuo of the right braid, pick up three 11º seed beads. Sew back down through the second hole of the last regular SuperDuo on the left braid **(m)**.

Sew down through the left hole of the next Mini SuperDuo. Continue following this thread path through the regular SuperDuos and Mini SuperDuos on the left side and finish off the thread by tying a few half-hitch knots. Transfer the needle to the 8" tail, pick up three 11º seed beads, and sew into the second hole of the last regular SuperDuo on the left braid. Continue sewing into the row of beads and finish off the thread with a couple of half-hitch knots. Trim the thread tails.

Finishing

Bind each braid ⅛" past the beads. Trim the excess braid and glue an endcap to each braid. Be sure to situate each end-cap so its ring is parallel to the bracelet. Allow to dry for 24 hours. Use jump rings to attach the clasps **(n)**.

Square
BRAID

Kaku Yatsu

The square braid sequence looks very similar to the basketweave at first glance: both are comprised of one clockwise round followed by a counter-clockwise round. Look closely though and you'll see the differences. First of all, the square braid starts with two empty spaces between the South warps. Also, rather than jumping every move, we're alternating between scooting and jumping. What's the difference between a scoot and a jump, you ask? When you scoot, you don't cross over any other warp.

This braid is called *Kaku Yatsu* in Japanese. *Kaku* is square and *Yatsu* is eight, so this is an eight-warp square braid.

Midnight's
Treasure
Necklace

This is my favorite color layout for the square braid for two reasons: First, with this arrangement you'll do all of the clockwise moves with one color and all of the counter-clockwise moves with the other. That's a big advantage when learning a new braid structure. Second, the layout is very slimming (you know what they say about vertical stripes). The square braid is narrow to begin with, and this color pattern accentuates that characteristic.

Set Up

Cut eight 54" pieces of satin cord. Tie them together using an overhand knot. Lock in the warps in place **(a)**. Notice the gaps at the bottom of the disk: they're important. Make sure your set-up matches the picture. This is the standard starting position for a square braid. Wind each warp onto a bobbin and clip the center weight below the knot.

Braiding Mantra: "Scoot. Jump Two." Use your right hand to pick up the top-right color A warp (red in the example photos) and scoot it around clockwise so it is above the warps on the right-hand side of the disk **(b)**. Notice when a warp scoots, it doesn't jump over any other warp. Use your right hand to pick up the adjacent color A warp (red). Moving clockwise, jump over the next two color B warps (blue) and lock in place to the right of the color A warp at the bottom **(c)**.

Yes, we want to jump into the gap. You're right. That was a big no-no in the basketweave, but it's correct in the square braid.

➤ Supplies

Kumihimo Toolkit
- standard thickness disk
- **8** plain bobbins
- 90g center weight

Other Materials
- 2mm satin cord
  - 6 yd. color A
  - 6 yd. color B
- **2** 5–6mm endcaps
- endcap with 5mm or larger bail

Finished Necklace Length: 24"

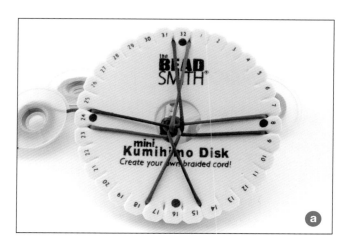

1 → 7

8 → 17

Wrong! You only jumped one warp.

Close, but not quite. Move one space to the left so that your same color warps are next to each other.

18 → 23

Tips for Learning the Square Braid

- The braiding sequence is composed of two rounds: first clockwise, then counter-clockwise.
- Hang on tight if you get lost! The next warp to move is always adjacent to the warp you just placed.
- Always reposition the warps before starting the next sequence. That means closing the side gaps and making a gap at the bottom.

24 → 1

Now that we're at the bottom of the disk, we're going to switch hands. Hold the disk with your right hand and use your left hand to pick up the adjacent color A warp. Scoot clockwise and lock in place just below the warps on the left side of the disk **(d)**.

Use your left hand to pick up the adjacent color A warp. Jump over the next two color B warps (blue) and lock in place to the right of the top warp **(e)**. That's it for the clockwise round. Keep your left hand at the top of the disk so it's in position for the counter-clockwise round. We'll be moving color B for this portion of the sequence.

32 → 26

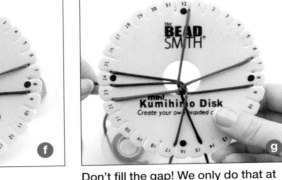

Don't fill the gap! We only do that at the bottom of the disk.

25 → 16

15 → 10

9 → 32

26 → 25, 23 → 24, 7 → 8, 10 → 9

17 → 18, 16 → 15

Hold the disk with your right hand and use your left hand to pick up the top-left color B warp. Moving counter-clockwise, scoot around and lock in place just above the warps on the left of the disk (f, g).

Use your left hand to pick up the adjacent color B warp. Moving counter-clockwise, jump over the next two color A warps and lock in place to the left of the color B warp at the bottom—filling the gap (h).

We're switching hands again since we're at the bottom of the disk. Use your left hand to hold the disk and pick up the adjacent color B warp with your right hand. Scoot counter-clockwise and lock in place just below the warps on the right side of the disk (i).

Use your right hand to pick up the adjacent color B warp and jump over the next two color A warps. Lock in place to the left of the top warp (j). This is the end of the sequence. Before we can repeat the sequence, we need to reset the disk. The top is fine; you can

leave it alone. Close the gaps on the left and right sides by moving each warp one slot closer to the dots (k). Make a gap at the bottom by moving each warp one slot away from the dot (l).

Notice how your colors are now arranged just as they were at the very start? That's unique to the two-color starting layout we used. It makes it easier to spot mistakes when you're learning, because if your colors are out of order when you go to begin the sequence again, you know right away a mistake was made in the last sequence. Carefully unbraid to find and correct your mistake. If you're using more than two colors or your two colors are arranged differently at the start, they'll move around each time and take four sequences to return to start.

Keep braiding until you reach the end of your cords. Remove the braid from the disk and knot the end. Bind and cut the braid to your desired length. Slide the pendant onto the middle of the braid. Glue an endcap to each end. Allow to dry for 24 hours.

About Tension

If your braid has excessive twisting, it means you're pulling harder in one direction than the other. This usually improves with practice and being conscious of how hard you pull with each hand.

Stretch Goal
Bracelet

Creative Closure!

I get a lot of "what if" questions when I'm teaching. "What if I braid with this? What if I do that instead?" If I know the answer, I'm happy to share, but frequently my response is, "I don't know. Try it and let me know what happens." I ask myself these questions all the time because experimenting is part of the fun of kumihimo. This bracelet is the answer to two questions: What else can I braid with? And how can I make a kumihimo bracelet that just rolls on?

Set Up and Braiding

Cut four 45" pieces of jewelry tube. Bind them together in the center for a "no-knot start." Holding the bound center of the cords over the hole in the disk, lock the warps in place in the standard starting position for an eight-warp square braid. Braid using the square braid moves. When finished, remove the braid from the disk and knot the end. Bind and cut the braid to the desired length, keeping in mind the length your focal bead will add (my focal bead is ⅞" long and I cut my braid 7" long). Glue on endcaps and allow to dry.

Creative Closure: Secret Stretch

The braided rubber tubing is a little stretchy on its own, but we're going to add a secret extra stretchy spot by joining the two endcaps together using some beads on stretchy cord. Cut a 15" piece of stretchy cord. Fold it in half and attach it to one of the endcaps using a lark's head knot. To make a lark's head knot, put the folded end of the stretchy cord through the ring on the endcap. Then pass the tails through the folded end **(a)**.

Thread both pieces of stretchy cord onto a big-eye needle. Pick up a 6º seed bead, a focal bead, and a 6º. Pass through the loop on the other endcap twice, pulling the beads snugly between the endcaps so there aren't any gaps **(b)**.

Pass back through all three beads again and pull snugly. Pass through the endcap loop and back through one seed bead. Tie a half-hitch knot. Pass through the focal bead and then tie another half-hitch knot. Put a dab of Hypo-Cement on each knot and then trim the tails.

➤ Supplies

Kumihimo Toolkit
- standard thickness disk
- **8** plain bobbins
- **90g** center weight

Other Materials
- 5 yd. jewelry tube, 2mm diameter
- 7mm endcaps
- focal bead
- .5mm stretchy cord
- Hypo Cement

Finished Bracelet Length:
approx. 9½" (fits 7" wrist)

Sizing

This bracelet sits loosely on the wrist similar to a bangle, but because it stretches it doesn't have to be entirely large enough to fit over your hand. My 9" bracelet stretches enough to fit over a 10" hand.

Crystal Morning
Necklace

Creative Closure !

➤ Supplies

Kumihimo Toolkit
- standard thickness disk
- **8** plain bobbins
- 45g center weight

Other Materials
- 6 yd. Ondule ribbon
- 12 yd. twisted metallic thread
- pendant with 3.5mm or larger bail
- 2' 22-gauge round silver-plated wire
- lobster claw or clasp of your choice
- **2** jump rings to attach the clasp

Finished Necklace Length:
approx. 22½"

Sometimes a necklace design starts with the pendant, and sometimes it starts with the fiber. This piece started with a beautiful skein of variegated Ondule ribbon with just a touch a rainbow metallic edging. I wanted to bring out a little more sparkle, so I decided to combine the ribbon with metallic threads. Combining thick and thin fibers in this way changes the texture of the braid so it ripples slightly on the surface.
I searched a long time before finding just the right pendant for my braid, but when I saw this wire-wrapped crystal, I knew it was the one. Wire-wrapped endcaps complete the design and echo the pendant.

Ondule ribbon is about ¼" wide, has a somewhat wavy appearance, and is available with and without metallic edging.

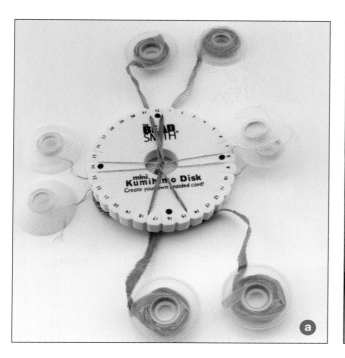

Set Up

For this braid, half of the warps will be a single piece of Ondule ribbon and half the warps will be two pieces of metallic thread. Cut four 54" pieces of Ondule ribbon and eight 54" pieces of metallic thread. Tie all 12 pieces together at one end using an overhand knot. Using the standard starting position for a square braid (see p. 61), lock the Ondule ribbon in the north and south positions, and lock the metallic threads in the east and west positions. Remember there will be two pieces of metallic thread in each horizontal position **(a)**.

Braid using the square braid moves. When finished, remove the braid from the disk and tie an overhand knot at the end. Bind each end of the braid to your desired length using a 24" piece of thread. Don't cut the tails after binding.

Whip Stitch the Bindings

Thread a #10 beading needle on the longer binding tail and sew your way completely around the binding twice using whip stitches. To make a whip stitch, put your needle into the braid just below the binding. Exit the braid just above the binding **(b)**.

Scoot down 2mm and repeat. The stitches always start below the binding and end above the binding (overhand knot side). Tie off the ends of the thread and trim the tails close. Repeat for the other binding. Cut the braid very close to the bindings and slide the pendant to the middle of the braid.

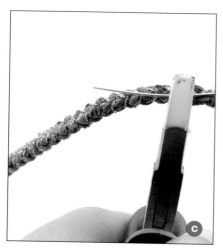

Creative Closure: Wire-Wrapping the Braid

Cut 12" of wire. Use flatnose or chain-nose pliers to hold the end of the wire firmly against the braid about ¼" from the end of the braid **(c)**.

About 1" of wire is the tail and the rest of the wire will be your working piece. Wrap the wire firmly around the braid, keeping the wraps right next to each other and evenly sized **(d)**.

When you reach the end of the braid, taper the wraps so they get tighter and cover most of the end of the braid **(e)**.

Use chainnose pliers to bend the wire at a right angle about ⅛" above the end of the braid. Make a wrapped loop.

Make a Decorative Spiral

Trim the remaining wire so it is 1" long. Use roundnose pliers to make a small loop at the very end of the wire **(f)**.

Use flatnose pliers to hold the loop with your dominant hand. Use the thumb of your non-dominant hand to apply pressure to the wire where it exits the loop. Keep this pressure firm as you rotate the loop using your dominant hand. Guide the wire around the loop to form a spiral **(g)**.

Press the spiral down against the wire-wrapped endcap. Trim any tail wire from the start of the endcap.

Repeat for the other end of the necklace.

Assembly

Use jump rings to attach a clasp half to each end of the necklace.

Bridge
Bracelet

The shape of the square braid really lends itself to framing beads. Size 3º seed beads are great to work with because they have large holes to accommodate multiple thread passes and your aim doesn't need to be great when stitching. If you have trouble finding 3ºs, try scaling down the project and using 1mm satin cord with 6º seed beads.

➤ Supplies

Kumihimo Toolkit
- standard thickness disk
- **8** plain bobbins
- 90g center weight

Other Materials
- 12 yd. 2mm satin cord
- 8–10g 3º seed beads
- beading thread to match satin cord color
- **2** 10.7x7mm endcaps
- magnetic clasp
- **2** jump rings to attach clasp

Finished Bracelet Length:
approx. 7½" (fits 6½" wrist)

Set Up

Cut eight 54" pieces of satin cord. Tie them together using an overhand knot and lock in place on the disk using the standard starting position for a square braid (see p. 61). Braid a square braid until you reach the end of the cords. Remove from the disk and tie the end using an overhand knot.

Prepare a Thread for Stitching

Cut 54" of beading thread. Try to match the color as much as possible to your braid. Tie an overhand knot at one end, wrapping the tail through the loop twice before closing the loop. This will make your knot a bit bigger. Trim the tail right next to the knot. Thread a #10 beading needle on the other end of the thread.

We're going to fold the braid in half and sew some large seed beads in between the two braid halves (see Alternative Starting Method, next page). Don't be afraid! This is easier than you think, even if you don't have a lot of stitching experience. The secret to hiding the stitches is to find the low spots in the braid. Take a look at your square braid. Do you see how the cords line up in little V shapes? The pointy part of the V is the low spot. Aim your needle there **(a)**.

If you make your stitches by sewing through the low spot, the stitches will disappear inside the braid. Try to hit the low spot both as your needle enters and exits the braid. (There are low spots on all sides of the braid.) If you feel a lot of resistance when you try to push your

needle through, you've hit the cotton core at the center of the satin cord. Pull out, reposition, and try again. To secure the beads in place, pass through each bead four times before moving on to the next bead. (I find it helpful to count the passes as I work.)

Adding Beads

Ready? Let's go! Fold the braid in half so it is U-shaped. I'm right handed, so I find it most comfortable to work from right to left with the open legs of the U pointing to the left. From here on out, I'll be referring to the top braid and the bottom braid. Those are the two legs of the same folded braid. Sew up through the top braid from the inside of the U to the outside of the U about ¼" down from the fold **(b)**.

This will position the knot on the inside of the "U" where it won't be visible. Turn around and sew back through the top braid in the very same spot. Re-entering the braid in the same place where you exited will keep the stitch as small as possible. Now the working thread is on the inside of the U and it is exiting the top braid very near the knot. Pick up a seed bead with your needle and let it slide down the thread so it is sitting against the braid (first pass). Nestle the bead into the fold. Sew down through the bottom braid **(c)**.

Turn around and sew up through the bottom braid in the same spot, passing up through the bead (second pass) and up through the top braid **(d)**.

Turn around and sew down through the top braid in the very same spot. Continue passing through the bead (third pass) and down through the bottom braid. Turn around and sew up through the bottom braid in the same spot. Continue up through the bead (fourth pass) and up through the top braid. Turn around and sew down through just the top braid in the same spot **(e)**.

That bead is secure! Don't sew into it again.

Pick up a new bead (first pass). Snuggle it next to the previous bead. Sew down through the bottom braid **(f)**.

ALTERNATIVE STARTING METHOD
Rather than folding the one long braid in half, you could bind and cut the braid in two. Another option would be to start with two bracelet-length braids.

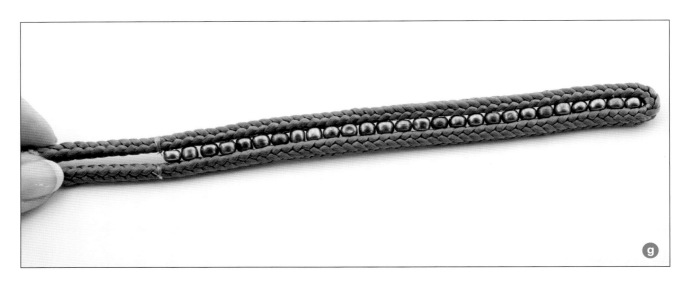

Turn around and sew up through the bottom braid in the same spot, passing up through the bead (second pass) and up through the top braid. Turn around and sew down through the top braid in the very same spot. Continue passing through the bead (third pass) and down through the bottom braid. Turn around and sew up through the bottom braid in the same spot. Continue up through the bead (fourth pass) and up through the top braid. Turn around and sew down through the top braid in the same spot. That bead is secure! Don't sew into it again.

Keep adding beads until you reach your desired length. Depending on your bracelet length, you may need to finish off your working thread and add a new one. This is far easier than trying to work with an extra-long piece of thread.

To finish the thread, tie a half-hitch knot around one of the threads connecting a bead to the braid. Sew through the bead and through the braid. Trim the thread as it comes out of the braid. If you need to add more thread, start a new one as you did at the beginning of the bracelet.

When you are finished adding beads, bind each braid very close to the last bead **(g)**.

Trim the excess braid and glue on an endcap. The folded end of the braid doesn't need binding—just glue the endcap on. Allow to dry for 24 hours and then attach a clasp using jump rings.

16-Warp Hollow BRAID

Naiki Gumi

More warps! More fun! The hollow braid is based on the same movement pattern as the basketweave braid, but with twice as many warps. You'll notice right away how this braid gets its name—there's an unmistakable indent at the point of braiding that quickly becomes a hole as you braid. You have two options when designing with the hollow braid: braid around some sort of core to stabilize the braid or leave it empty and enjoy it as a flat braid.

This braid is called *Naiki Gumi* in Japanese. The *Gumi* part is easy. That means braid. The meaning of *Naiki* (pronounced like the shoe) is less clear. The braid is probably named for an Edo period braiding machine called a Naikidai, but it's not clear how the machine got its name.

Check Me Out

Necklace & Bracelet

Be sure you've had a lot of practice with the eight-warp basketweave before moving on to the 16-warp variation. We're going to try out both versions of the hollow braid in this lovely set. For the necklace, you'll braid around a core that keeps the braid plump and round, but for the bracelet, you let the hollow braid flatten out. Same braid. Two very different looks!

➤ Supplies

Kumihimo Toolkit
- standard thickness disk
- **16** plain bobbins
- 90g center weight

Other Materials
- 2mm satin rattail
  - 6 yd. color A
  - 3 yd. color B
  - 1½ yd. color C
  - 1½ yd. color D
- 8" 6mm outside diameter plastic tubing (I used aquarium tubing)
- **2** 10mm endcaps for the necklace
- **2** 8mm endcaps for the bracelet

- pendant with 10mm or larger bail
- **2** sets of toggle clasps
- 10" chain
- **7** 4mm 20-gauge jump rings

Finished Necklace Length:
approx. 19½"

Finished Bracelet Length:
approx. 7" (fits 6½" wrist)

Note: Colors B, C, and D should all be shades of the same color (blue in the example).

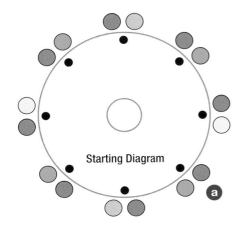

Starting Diagram

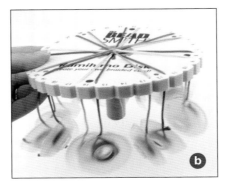

32 → 3

4 → 7

8 → 11

Set Up

Cut eight 54" pieces of satin cord. Bind them together in the center for a "no-knot start." Holding the bound center of the cords over the hole in the disk, follow the starting diagram to lock the warps in place in the standard starting position for a 16-warp hollow braid **(a)**. Wind each warp onto a bobbin and attach the center weight **(b)**.

Keep in mind this braid structure is just like the eight-warp basketweave, except this time we have 16 warps. Before starting, make sure your color arrangement matches the starting diagram so your main color (gray) and your accent color (shades of blue) alternate around the disk. With this color arrangement, the gray will do all of the clockwise moves and the blue will do all of the counter-clockwise moves.

We'll be working clockwise for the first round. Use your right hand to lift the top-left warp out of its slot; it's gray in the example photos. Moving clockwise, jump over the neighboring warp and lock it above the next group of warps **(c)**.

Use your right hand to pick up the adjacent warp; it's also gray. Moving clockwise, lock it above the next group of warps **(d)**.

Keep going. Do more of the same. Use your right hand to pick up the adjacent warp. Moving clockwise, lock it above the next group of warps **(e)**.

Use your right hand to pick up the adjcent warp. Moving clockwise, lock it to the right of the bottom group of warps **(f)**.

Great! We've made it halfway around the disk. Now it's time to switch hands. Hold the disk with your right hand and use your left hand to move the warps. We're still working with the gray warps, so take the middle warp from the bottom group and moving clockwise, lock it below the next group of warps **(g)**.

Use your left hand to pick up the adjacent warp; you guessed it—gray. Moving clockwise, lock it below the next group of warps **(h)**.

Still using your left hand, pick up the adjacent warp. Moving clockwise, lock it below the next group of warps **(i)**.

12 → 15

16 → 19

20 → 23

24 → 27

TIPS FOR LEARNING THE HOLLOW BRAID

- Use a ball-point pen to add four extra dots to the face of your disk to show where the warp pairs reset and the end of the sequence. Add a dot to each of these places: between slot 4 and 5, between slot 12 and 13, between slot 20 and 21, and between 28 and 29.
- Use a 6" disk so the bobbins have more room and tangle less.

28 → 32

1 → 30

29 → 26

25 → 22

21 → 18

17 → 14

Almost there! One more this direction! Use your left hand to take the adjacent warp, jump over its neighbor and place it to the left of the very top warp **(j)**.

Now we're going to complete the sequence by doing a round of counter-clockwise moves. Use your left hand to pick up the top-right warp; it's blue in the example photos. Moving counter-clockwise, lock it above the next group of warps **(k)**.

Use your left hand to pick up the adjacent warp; it's also blue. Moving counter-clockwise, jump over one warp and lock it above the next group of warps **(l)**.

Keep moving counter-clockwise and use your left hand to pick up the adjacent blue warp, jump over one gray warp, and lock in place above the next blue warp **(m)**.

Use your left hand to pick up the adjacent blue warp, jump over one gray warp, and lock in place to the left of the next blue warp **(n)**.

This is where we switch hands. Hold the disk with your left hand and use your right hand to pick up the adjacent blue warp. Moving counter-clockwise, jump over the next gray warp and lock in place below the next blue warp **(o)**.

13 → 10

9 → 6

5 → 1

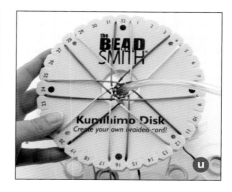

Use your right hand to pick up the adjacent blue warp, jump over one warp and lock in place below the next blue warp **(p)**.

Moving counter-clockwise, use your right hand to lift the adjacent blue warp, jump over the gray warp, and lock in place below the next blue warp **(q)**.

Ok, last one! Use your right hand to lift the adjacent blue warp, jump over the gray warp, and lock to the right of the very top warp **(r)**.

Well that's the sequence for the hollow braid. It takes longer to read it than to do it. It's lots of moves, but each move is really the same. Just jump over one warp. Be sure to reset the disk to the starting position before beginning the sequence again. You do this by scooting each warp one spot closer to a dot to close up all the gaps you made while braiding **(s)**.

After braiding about five sequences, you can see a well is forming at the point of braiding **(t)**.

This is where we'll add the core. Cut an 8" piece of plastic tubing and shove it down into the braid **(u)**. From here on out, we'll be braiding around the tubing. Conveniently, it's stiff enough to stay up and out of the way for the most part, but you may need to hold it in place for a few sequences early on.

As you braid, the tubing will be completely covered by the fiber and won't be visible. Once you reach the end of the tubing, braid for at least another inch if you just want to make the necklace or until the end of the cords if you're making the bracelet, also. When finished braiding, remove the braid from the disk and tie an overhand knot. Bind tightly just past the core. If making the bracelet, bind two more times on the flat part of the braid, once at each end of your desired bracelet length.

Finishing the Necklace

Slide your bail onto the necklace (the part with the core) and then glue a 10mm endcap to each end of the braid. Allow to dry. Attach 5½" of chain to each endcap using a small jump ring. Attach one half of a toggle clasp to each loose end of chain using a small jump ring.

Finishing the Bracelet

Glue an 8mm endcap onto each end of the flat braid. I just fold the flat braid onto itself to help it fit in the round endcaps. Allow to dry. Attach a toggle clasp using small jump rings.

➤ Supplies

Kumihimo Toolkit
- standard thickness disk
- **16** plain bobbins
- 90g center weight

Other Materials
- flat silk ribbon, about 7mm wide
  - 27 yd. color A
  - 9 yd. color B
  - 9 yd. color C
  - 3 yd color D
- Fray Check (optional)

Finished Length: approx. 60",
plus 6" tassel on each end

Creative Closure

Silk Ribbon
Lariat

Set Up and Braiding

Cut sixteen 3-yd. pieces of ribbon. Tie them together 6" from one end using an overhand knot. Lock in place on the disk using the standard starting position for a 16-warp hollow braid (see p. 76) **(a)**.

Clip a heavy gator weight just below the knot and braid using the hollow braid move sequence. As your braid gets longer and longer, tie knots in it so your center weight continues to hang freely without resting on your lap. Keep an eye on how much ribbon remains on each warp and stop when you have about 6" left on your shortest warp.

Your braid will be about 60" long at that point. Remove the braid from the disk and tie an overhand knot. Relax the braid by stretching it end to end.

Creative Closure: Tassels

Trim the tassels so they're both similar in length. (Since the ribbon is a bit crinkly, don't worry about getting each piece of ribbon in the tassel exactly the same length. So long as they're close, the variation in lengths adds a bohemian flair.) The silk ribbon generally keeps a clean-cut edge, but you can treat the ends with Fray Check or a similar product, if desired.

A B
B A
A B
C A
A C
D A
A A
C A

Starting Diagram

(a)

How to Wear the Lariat

- For a long, lean look, drape the lariat around your neck with one tassel slightly lower than the other. Grab both ends of the lariat near your belly button and tie an overhand knot.
- For a higher focal point, fold the lariat in half and center it behind your neck. Pull the tassel ends through the folded side.
- As a belt, tie the lariat around your waist using a square knot. Position the knot off-center, closer to your hip than your belly button.

TIP

I used hand-dyed, variegated silk ribbon for this versatile lariat that can be worn as either a necklace or a belt.

When working with flat ribbon, it will naturally want to twist up or fold when you lock it in the slots on the disk. Just let it. There's no need to try to keep it flat; it's a lot of work that won't change your finished product.

My Garden
Bracelet

At first glance, you may think the flowers are riveted to the braid, but it's really easier than that! They're actually held in place with headpins. The secret is the flat spacer bead on the back. Using a 4" disk for this project will let you get the maximum braid length from your leather.

➤ **Supplies**

Kumihimo Toolkit
• standard-thickness disk
• 90g center weight

Other Materials
• 1.5mm leather cord
  - 12' color A
  - 4' color B
  - **5** 2" copper headpins
  - **3** 7–8mm flat spacer beads
• enameled copper flowers with center holes in assorted colors
  - 34mm flower
  - 22mm flower
  - 17mm flower
  - **3** 12mm flowers
  - **2** 12mm flower caps (endcap alternative 10mm round)
  - **4** O beads or 8° seed beads (if using flower caps)
• 14mm magnetic endcap
• 4mm jump rings to attach the clasp

Finished Bracelet Length: approx. 8½", including endcaps and clasp (fits up to a 7" wrist)

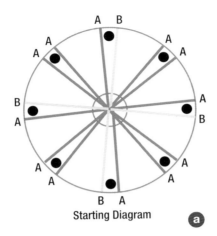

Starting Diagram

Set Up

Cut eight 24" pieces of leather (six color A and two color B) using craft scissors (see Sizing Chart, p. 85). Don't ruin your good kumihimo scissors cutting leather! Line up the ends and bind the eight pieces together in the middle for a "no-knot start." Hold the binding over the hole in the disk and arrange the cords following the starting diagram **(a)**.

For the smoothest start, try to arrange the warps so the opposite ends of a piece of leather are 180 degrees from each other. For example, the warps in positions 1 and 17 are the same piece of leather **(b)**.

The cords are so short you can easily skip using bobbins for this project. Clip on a heavy center weight and braid using the 16-warp hollow braid sequence. Don't worry if it looks a little wide and spread out at first. It takes several sequences for the braid to start moving downward. As you braid, push the point of braiding down into the hole every few sequences **(c)**.

Braid until one piece of leather is too short to lock into the disk. Before removing the braid from the disk, prepare a piece of binding thread. Holding the braid below the disk at the point of braiding, remove each piece of leather from its slot. Bind the end of the braid. Don't worry about length at this point. We're just binding to keep it from unraveling right now.

With the braid securely off the disk, flatten it out with your fingers and bind again for your desired length. Keep in mind the flower endcaps and clasp will add about 2".

Drop one of the flat spacers onto a headpin and push the headpin through the center of the braid **(d)**.

The flat spacer will sit against the back of the braid and keep the headpin from pulling through.

NOTE

The spacer really does need to be at least 7mm across. I tried it with a 6mm spacer and it pulled right through the braid.

Saving two of the smallest flowers for later, stack four flowers on the headpin, starting with the largest and finishing with the smallest. Hold everything in place and trim the headpin ½" above the smallest flower **(e)**.

Use roundnose pliers to roll the headpin down towards the flowers **(f)**.

Keep rolling until the flowers feel tight enough to not slide around **(g)**.

Measure 1¼" from the center of the stack of flowers and add one small flower using the same process. Repeat for the other side **(h, i)**.

Stack a seed bead, a flower cap, and a seed bead on a headpin and make a wrap loop. The seed bead or O bead

will keep the headpin from pulling through **(j)**.

Do this again with the other flower cap. Attach the clasp to the wire-wrapped flower cap with jump rings **(k)**.

When I glue on endcaps, usually I do both sides at once, but the leather in the loose braid is really springy, so I do only one side at a time. After the first side has dried a few hours, then I move on to the other side. Use craft scissors to trim the excess leather close to one of the bindings. Glue on an endcap. Because the flower caps are a tad big for the braid, I hold the flower cap in place for about 10 minutes before setting it down to dry. This gives the glue a chance

to set up and ensures the cap is on straight. Wait a few hours and then repeat for the other side of the bracelet. Allow both sides to dry for 24 hours before wearing.

TIP
If you prefer a snugger fit for your endcaps, try 10mm rounds. No special handling is required. Just trim the braid and glue as usual.

Sizing Chart

This bracelet is thick and springy, so it will need to be longer than your wrist size in order to fit properly. Plan on making the braid, itself, long enough to fit all the way around your wrist. The endcap and clasp will add the length to account for the springiness. Of course, if your braid ends up a bit longer than you need, you can always cut it down to size. That's what I did with mine.

How long should I cut my leather?

Braid Length	Warp Length	Cut 8 pieces each this long	Total Needed For Bracelet
6"	10.5"	21"	14'
7"	12"	24"	16'
8"	14"	28"	18' 8"
9"	15.5"	30"	20'

Kumihimo Math

The usual 3-to-1 rule is excessive on this springy leather braid. Starting with 12" per warp (that's eight 24" pieces because we're using a no-knot start), I got a braid 7" long. When you divide 12 by 7, you get 1.71. That's our usage multiplier. If you wanted to make a longer braid (let's say an 8" bracelet), take your finished length and multiply by 1.7. So 8 x 1.7 = 13.68". Round up to the nearest half inch, and you have 14" for each warp. Multiply by 2 for the "no-knot start," and for your 8" bracelet you would cut eight 28" pieces of leather.

The Ombraid
Bracelet

You're loving the hollow braid, right? You've made several in all sorts of color combinations and you've even mastered a solid-color version. You know this braid forwards and back. You can even unbraid it while watching TV! Then you're ready for this. You're ready for the OMBRAID!

You're going to learn two neat tricks in this project: working around a soft core and changing colors mid-braid! If you'll recall from the "Check Me Out Necklace," p. 74, when working around a stiff core like rubbing tubbing, the core just stands up in the middle of the braid and you can easily work around it. When working with a soft core, we'll tie an extension cord and a weight to it so we can toss it over our shoulder or around our neck. We'll be working with the numbers a lot in the project, so be sure to work number side up on your disk. Remember the number is printed to the *right* of the slot it refers to.

This is a challenging project that will test your understanding of the point of braiding. Read all the way through the instructions before you start.

➤ Supply List
Kumihimo Toolkit
- **17** plain bobbins (that's not a typo— you need an extra bobbin)
- 90g center weight
- 45g center weight (Yep, you need both weights.)
- 1–1½-yd. scrap rattail, any size or color (this will be used as a tool)
- tweezers or awl
- 2mm satin cord
  - 12 yd. color A (green)
  - 12 yd. color B (black)
- 10mm magnetic endcap

Finished Bracelet Length:
approx. 8" (fits 6" wrist)

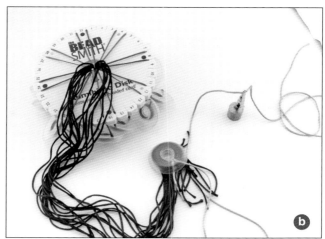

Set Up

Cut eight 54" pieces of color A satin and eight 54" pieces of color B satin. Bind the middle of all 16 pieces together for a "no-knot start." Lock the color A warps on the disk using the standard starting position for a 16-warp hollow braid (see p. 76). Wind each color A warp onto a bobbin. Clip the heavy weight to the start of the braid below the disk. The sixteen pieces of color B satin cord will be the core for now. They are on top of the disk but not locked into slots **(a)**.

Tie the scrap rattail onto a plain bobbin. Wind the last few inches of the color B cords onto the bobbin. Clip the lite weight onto the middle of the satin scrap **(b)**.

Gently toss the weight over your shoulder or around your neck **(c)**. This will pull the core upward and hold it out of the way while you work. Don't let the core pull up so hard the point of braiding lifts off the disk. Braid using the 16-warp hollow braid sequence. Work around the core. Braid 4" of solid color before beginning the transition.

Transitioning

Let's start by taking a closer look at the path warp 1 takes from the point of braiding (POB) to the slot at the edge of the disk. It begins by passing under warp 16. Next, it passes over warp 12 and under warp 8. It then passes over warp 4 before locking into the disk **(d)**. All of the counter-clockwise warps follow

this same under, over, under, over pattern as they travel from the POB to the slot (the position numbers of the warps will vary, of course). For clockwise warps, it's over, under, over, under.

The general concept here is that one by one, each cord that is currently part of the core will swap places with one of the warps. We'll transition two warps and then braid two sequences. Then we'll do the next two warps and so on. The trick to a smooth transition is for the new warp (the color B cord transitioning out of the core) to perfectly trace the path of the old warp (the color A cord that is transitioning to the core) from the POB to the slot. Things are pretty tight at the point of braiding, so we'll loosen some

of the other warps and use tweezers or an awl to help get the new warp into position. Once the new warp is in place, side-by-side with the old warp, we'll back the old warp out of the braid and add it to the core.

At the beginning of each transition step, remove the bobbins from the two warps that will be transitioning as well as the core bobbin. At the end of each step, replace all the bobbins and get the core into position over your shoulder before braiding again.

Transition Step 1
Start with warps 1 and 17.

Loosen warp 16 **(e)**, and thread a color B core piece under it **(f)**.

Retighten warp 16.
Next loosen warp 8 and thread the core piece over warp 12 and under warp 8 **(g)**. Retighten warp 8. Pass the color B core piece over warp 4 and lock it in slot 1 **(h)**.

Great! The color B core piece has made its way to the edge of the disk and is now the new warp for that slot. Now we have to get the old color A warp out of the braid and into the core. Remove the color A warp from slot 1 and pull it out from under warp 8 **(i)**.

Loosen warp 16 and pull the old color A warp out from under it **(j)**.

Retighten warp 16.

Bring the old color A warp into the center of the braid and let it hang out with the other core warps **(k)**.

Take a quick peek under the disk at the point of braiding. See how smooth and seamless the transition is **(l)**. Isn't this neat?

In turn, each warp will swap with a core piece using the same technique. I'll list the numbers in each step for those of you who find them helpful, but the most important thing is to just look closely at the point of braiding and observe how a warp makes it way out to the slot.

Now do warp 17 using the same technique. Its path is under warp 32, over warp 28, under warp 24, and over warp 20, lock into slot 17 **(m)**.

Braid two sequences.

Transition Step 2
The color B warps we transitioned last time have moved to slots 9 and 25, giving us new color A warps to transition in slots 1 and 17. Repeat transition step 1 **(n)**.

Transition Step 3
Transition warps 5 and 21 **(o)**.

The path for warp 5 is under warp 20, over warp 16, under warp 12, and over warp 8.

The path for warp 21 is under warp 4, over warp 32, under warp 28, and over warp 24.

Braid two sequences.

Transition Step 4
Repeat transition step 3 **(p)**.

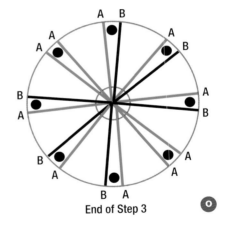

End of Step 3

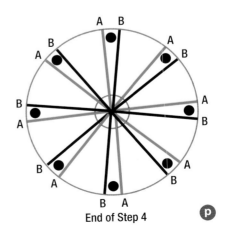

End of Step 4

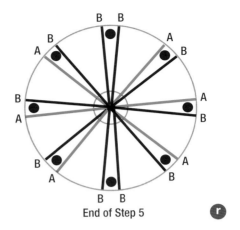

End of Step 5

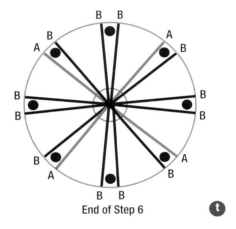

End of Step 6

Transition Step 5

Now that all of the counter-clockwise warps have transitioned, it's time to do the clockwise warps. To get the clockwise warps on top where they're easier to work with, braid the first half of a sequence (clockwise moves only) **(q)**. Close the gaps.

Transition warps 32 and 16 **(r)**.

The path for warp 32 is under warp 17, over warp 21, under warp 25, and over warp 29.

The path for warp 16 is under warp 1, over warp 5, under warp 9, and over warp 13.

Braid the second half of the sequence (counter-clockwise moves only) **(s)**. Close the gaps.

Braid one sequence.

Transition Step 6

Repeat transition step 5 **(t)**.

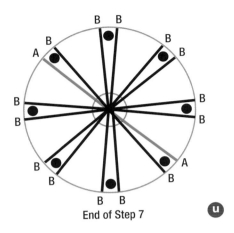

End of Step 7

Transition Step 7

Braid the first half of a sequence (clockwise moves only). Close the gaps.

Transition warps 4 and 20 **(u)**.

The path for warp 4 is under warp 21, over warp 25, under warp 29, and over warp 1.

The path for warp 20 is under warp 5, over warp 9, under warp 13, and over warp 17.

Braid the second half of the sequence (counter-clockwise moves only). Close the gaps.

Braid one sequence.

Transition Step 8

Repeat transition step 7 **(v)**. Yeah! High five! You did it! Transition completed. Take a look under the disk and admire your work **(w)**.

My transition is lumpy!

A lumpy transition is caused when you don't pull the old warp all the way back to the point of braiding as it transitions to the core.

That old teal warp needs to be pulled out from under two more turquoise warps before it can join the core.

Finishing

Braid around the core until you are out of material. Remove the braid from the disk and knot the end. Bind and cut the braid to your desired length. Glue on endcaps. Allow to dry for 24 hours.

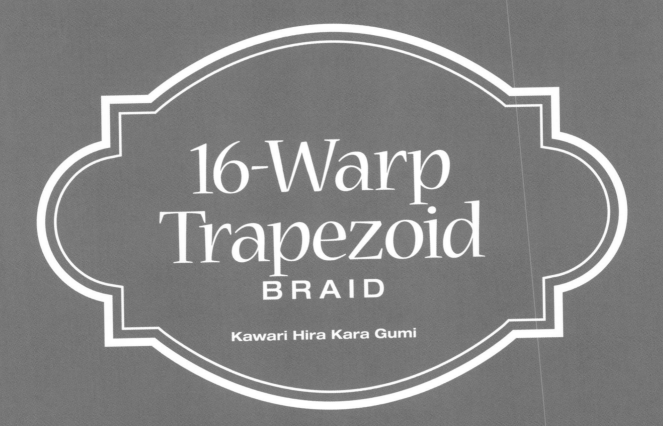

16-Warp Trapezoid
BRAID

Kawari Hira Kara Gumi

This is a 16-warp variation of the half-round braid. What's neat about doubling the number of warps is how dramatically the shape changes! What was mostly flat is now sturdy, thick, and has an interesting trapezoidal cross-section.

Ready for a long Japanese name? *Kawari Hira Kara Gumi*. Some of those words you already know. *Kara* is from China and *Gumi* is braid. *Hira* means flat and broad. *Kawari* is variation. So this very descriptive Japanese title means a variation of a flat braid from China.

Ancient Geometry

Necklace & Bracelet

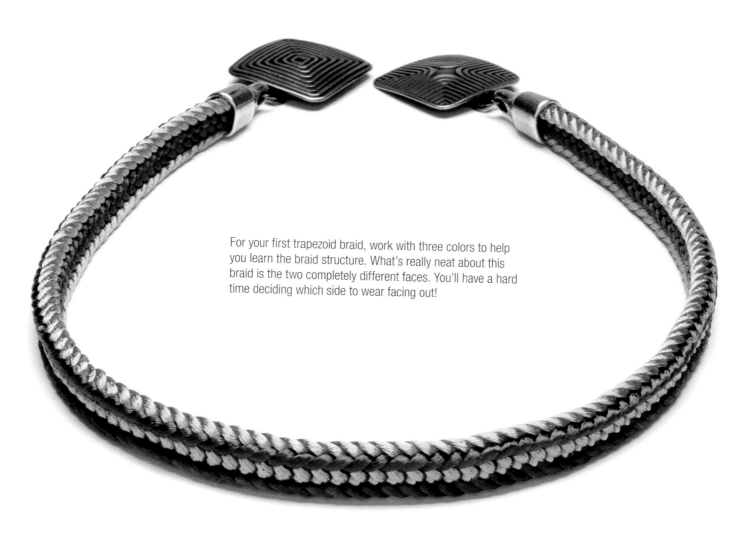

For your first trapezoid braid, work with three colors to help you learn the braid structure. What's really neat about this braid is the two completely different faces. You'll have a hard time deciding which side to wear facing out!

TIP

The magnetic clasp on the necklace is reversible, so it's perfect for this two-way braid. Wear the clasp in the front and it doubles as a pendant.

➤ Supply List

Kumihimo Toolkit
- standard thickness disk
- **16** plain bobbins
- 45g center weight

Other Materials
- 2mm satin rattail
  - 12 yd. color A
  - 6 yd. color B
  - 6 yd. color C

For the necklace
- 1–1½" magnetic focal clasp
- **4** 18-gauge 5mm jump rings

For the bracelet
2 10x7mm magnetic endcaps

Finished Necklace Length: 18½"

Finished Bracelet Length:
8¼" (fits 6½" wrist)

Set Up

Cut sixteen 54" pieces of satin rattail (eight color A, four color B, and four color C). Tie all sixteen pieces together at one end using an overhand knot. Lock in place on the disk **(a)**.

Wind each warp onto a bobbin. Attach the center weight below the knot.

Braiding

The moves for this braid are exactly like the eight-warp half-round braid (see p. 45). The only difference is there are more warps on the disk. Every sequence, the eight warps closest to the dots are going to move and we're going to just ignore the other eight warps. The braiding mantra you can chant to yourself while braiding is **"Inside to outside."**

Using your right hand, pick up the warp immediately to the left of the top-dot. Moving diagonally, place it just below the group of warps on the right side of the disk **(b)**.

Using your left hand, pick up the warp immediately to the right of the top-dot. Moving diagonally, place it just below the group of warps on the left side of the disk **(c)**.

32 → 11

1 → 22

17 → 6

16 → 27

8 → 14

25 → 19

Using your right hand, pick up the warp immediately to the left of the bottom-dot. Moving diagonally, place it just above the group of warps on the right side of the disk **(d)**.

Using your left hand, pick up the warp immediately to the right of the bottom dot. Moving diagonally, place it just above the group of warps on the left side of the disk **(e)**.

Take a look at the top and bottom of the disk. There aren't any warps touching the dots, so we know we're finished working with those positions for this sequence. That just leaves the sides. Whoa, that's a lot of warps! Six on the left and six on the right. Don't panic! Remember, it's "inside to outside" for this braid. We're only concerned with the four warps on the inside of the bunch that are touching the dots. The other warps are waiting patiently for their turns in future sequences.

Using your right hand, pick up the warp immediately above the right-dot. Moving downward, place it just to the right of the bottom-group. Remember to stay on the outside of the group **(f)**.

Using your left hand, pick up the warp immediately above the left-dot. Moving downward, place it just to the left of the bottom-group. Remember to stay on the outside of the group **(g)**.

9 → 3

24 → 30

Using your right hand, pick up the warp immediately below the right-dot. Moving upward, place it just to the right of the top-group. Remember to stay on the outside of the group **(h)**.

Using your left hand, pick up the warp immediately below the left-dot. Moving upward, place it just to the left of the top-group. Stay on the outside of the group **(i)**.

What's this big "X" doing on my braid?

It all comes back to our braiding mantra, "Inside to outside." What happened here is on the first two moves of the sequence, you moved the outer warps instead of the inner warps.

Carefully unbraid back to your mistake and correct it. Remember the first step in unbraiding is to make the gaps around each dot so you can continue the braid sequence in reverse.

Am I doing something wrong? My accent colors keep moving around.

Not all at! This is completely normal and just part of the braid sequence. It actually takes four complete sequences for your accent color warps to return to the original layout. Of course your main color warps are moving around just as much, but you don't notice because they're all the same color. Recognizing the possible correct color arrangements can be very helpful if you need to unbraid.

31 → 32, 30 → 31, 2 → 1, 3 → 2

7 → 8, 6 → 7, 10 → 9, 11 → 10

Well done! That's the end of the sequence. Before beginning the next sequence, close gaps by moving each warp one slot closer to the dots **(j, k, l, m)**.

Braid until one warp is too short to continue and then remove the braid from the disk and knot the end.

Measure the size of your endcaps and clasp. Then decide how long you'd like the necklace and bracelet to be. Bind the braid at your desired lengths. Cut the braid and glue on endcaps. Allow to dry for 24 hours. Use jump rings to attach the clasp to the endcaps on the necklace.

TIPS FOR LEARNING THE BRAID

- Only the eight warps touching the dots will move each sequence. The other eight warps just hang out and wait their turn.
- Alternate hands as you braid: right, left, right, left. This will help keep your braid even and smooth.
- Always take warps from the inside of a group and place them on the outside of a group.

15 → 16, 14 → 15, 18 → 17, 19 → 18

23 → 24, 22 → 23, 26 → 25, 27 → 26

Starting position

After one sequence

After two sequences

After three sequences

After four sequences

Bling *Bracelet*

When the 16-warp trapezoid braid is made using 1.5mm Chinese knotting cord, it creates a firm cord similar in size and shape to licorice leather. This happy coincidence opens up a vast collection of slider beads and endcaps to mix and match. 11x7mm slider beads are now being made from metal, glass, ceramic, and polymer clay in an exciting variety of styles.

Set Up and Braiding

Cut eight 48" pieces of knotting cord. Bind them together in the center for a "no-knot start." Holding the bound center of the cords over the hole in the disk, lock the warps in place in the standard starting position for a 16-warp trapezoid braid (see p. 95). Braid until you run out of cord. When finished, remove the braid from the disk and knot the end.

Slide the slider beads onto the braid starting at the finished end of the braid (the end without a knot). Make sure the wider face of the braid is on top. Magnet the two halves of the endcap set together and then slide the finished end of the braid into one end. Hold the braid against your wrist to determine the correct length. Bind the braid at the desired length. Glue an endcap to each end of the braid and allow to dry before wearing.

➤ Supply List
Kumihimo Toolkit
- standard thickness disk
- **16** plain bobbins
- 45g center weight

Other Materials
- 32' 1.5mm Chinese knotting cord
- assorted 11x7mm slider beads
- 11x7mm magnetic endcaps

Finished Bracelet Length:
approx. 7½" (fits 6½" wrist)

TIP
If crystals aren't your style, try using a bronze slider bead and coordinating endcaps instead.

The Waterfall
Necklace

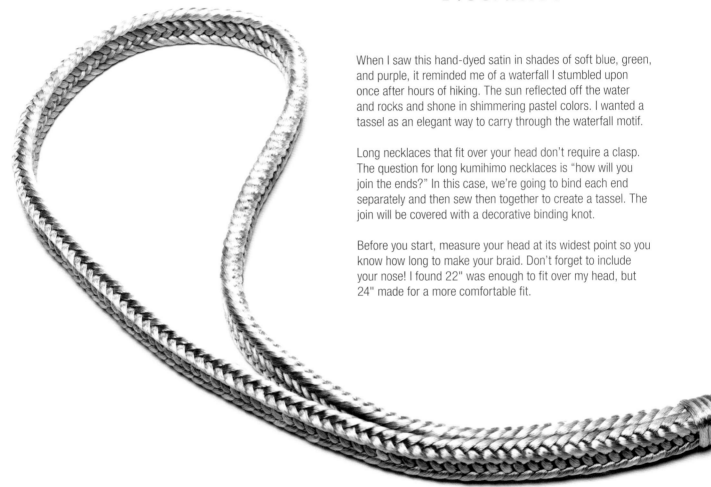

When I saw this hand-dyed satin in shades of soft blue, green, and purple, it reminded me of a waterfall I stumbled upon once after hours of hiking. The sun reflected off the water and rocks and shone in shimmering pastel colors. I wanted a tassel as an elegant way to carry through the waterfall motif.

Long necklaces that fit over your head don't require a clasp. The question for long kumihimo necklaces is "how will you join the ends?" In this case, we're going to bind each end separately and then sew then together to create a tassel. The join will be covered with a decorative binding knot.

Before you start, measure your head at its widest point so you know how long to make your braid. Don't forget to include your nose! I found 22" was enough to fit over my head, but 24" made for a more comfortable fit.

Set Up and Braiding

Cut sixteen 54" pieces of satin cord. Tie them together 4" from one end using an overhand knot. Lock in place on the disk using the standard starting position for a trapezoid braid (see p. 95). Wind each warp onto a bobbin. Clip a lite gator weight just below the knot **(a)** and begin braiding using the moves for a 16-warp trapezoid braid. Keep braiding until the braid is 25" long.

Finishing

When finished, remove the braid from the disk and knot the end. Bind each end of the braid using a 36" piece of beading thread. If possible, use a thread that color coordinates with the braid. Don't cut the tails after binding. On each binding, use the longer tail to sew the binding to the braid. Sew your way completely around the binding twice, using whip stitches. To make a whip stitch, put your needle into the braid just below the binding. Exit the braid just above the binding **(b)**.

Scoot down 2mm and repeat. The stitches always start below the binding (braid side) and end above the binding (overhand knot side). Tie off the ends of the thread and trim the tails close. Glue the bindings with Hypo Cement and allow to dry for 15 minutes.

Creative Closure: Making the Tassel

Untie the big overhand knots at the beginning and end of the braid so you have 16 tails of satin cord hanging loose at each end of the braid. These will become the tassel. When you look at your braid, you can see the two sides are different. One side is flatter and wider (top braid in the photo) and the other side is narrower and has two raised ridges (bottom braid in the photo) **(c)**.

➤ Supply List:

Kumihimo Toolkit
- standard thickness disk
- **16** plain bobbins
- 45g center weight

Other Materials
- 8" piece of satin cord in any color (this is a tool)
- 24 yd. 2mm hand-dyed satin cord
- Hypo Cement
- #10 long beading needle
- beading thread to match satin cord

Finished Necklace Length:
approx. 24", plus a 4" tassel

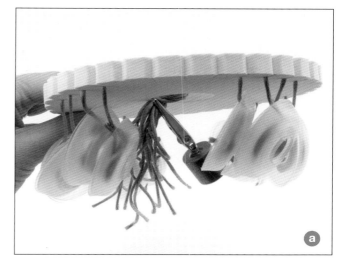

Creative Closure

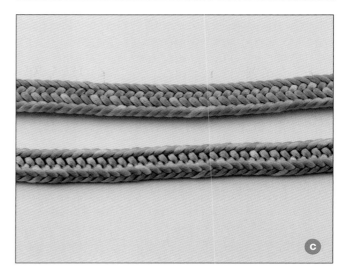

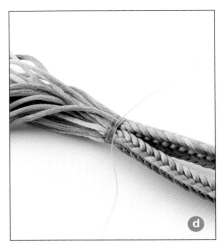

You can decide for yourself which side of the braid you'd like to face out in your necklace. The narrower side faces out in my necklace.

Cut a new 36" piece of thread. Line up the two ends of the braids at their bindings so that the wide sides of the braid are touching. Bind the two ends together **(d)**.

This new binding will be on top of the previous bindings. Make this binding about ⅜–¼" wide. Don't cut the tails after binding. Sew the two ends of the braid together by stitching straight through the braids **(e)**.

Make three or four stiches through the braids to secure. Tie the thread tails together and trim the tails close. Glue the binding with Hypo Cement and allow to dry for 15 minutes.

The 8" piece of satin cord is your knotting tool. Fold it in half. Set the knotting tool on top of the binding with the folded end towards the braid **(f)**.

The knotting tool is parallel to your braid. Holding the knotting tool in place with one hand, use your other hand to wrap the longest tassel cord around the bound braids and the knotting tool. Wrap towards the braid. Make the wraps firm, but not so tight as to compress the braid

Make four or five wraps around the braid, making sure to completely cover the binding and then bring the wrapping cord through the knotting tool **(g)**.

Holding the wraps in one hand, use your other hand to pull both tails of the knotting tool **(h)**.

This will pull the wrapping cord under the wraps. It may take some tugging to accomplish this. If it really won't go, you've wrapped too tightly. Unwrap it and try again. Put a dab of glue inside the decorative knot by working the needle tip of the Hypo Cement under the wraps **(i)**.

Try not to get any glue on the outside of the knot. Although Hypo Cement dries clear, it will leave what looks like a wet spot. Steam the tassel straight using either a clothing steamer or a pot of boiling water. If using boiling water, be very careful not to burn yourself and keep the tassel out of the water. Wrap the tassel in a piece of paper and cut straight through at your desired length.

Triple-Threat
Bracelet

This dainty braid takes some time to work up, but you'll be thrilled with the finished results. Lightweight and modern, the design is certainly eye-catching.

If you have a double-thick kumihimo disk, be sure to use it for this project. The double-thickness provides more surface area and friction for the wire and helps keep the tension even while you work. The beading wire is incredibly flexible and kink-resistant. I thought for sure it would kink up every time I locked it in a slot, but it held up great! The few kinks I did get were from transferring the wire from the spools it came from to the bobbins. (See Alternative Starting Method on p. 108.) Even those kinks weren't a big deal and are only visible under close examination.

➤ **Supply List**
Kumihimo Toolkit
- double-thickness disk
- **16** plain bobbins (for Alternative Starting Method)
- 45g center weight
- bead stopper
- hemostat

Other Materials
- mini spools of flexible beading wire (I used Soft Flex Medium)
  - **8** color A
  - **8** color B
- **2** 2.5mm x 15mm magnetic endcaps

Finished Bracelet Length:
approx. 6¾" (fits 6¼" wrist)

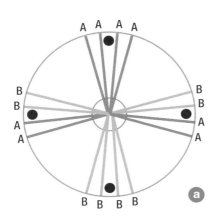

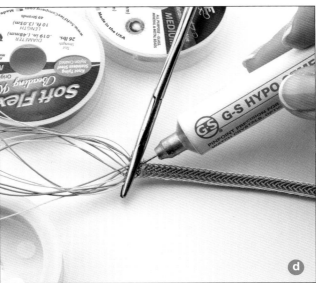

Sizing Your Bracelet

To make this triple-wide bracelet, we'll make a long braid and cut it into three pieces. Then we'll lay the three pieces side-by-side when gluing on the endcap. So, how long does our braid need to be? Use a tape measure to find your wrist size. Hold the tape measure as tightly or as loosely as you'd like the bracelet to fit, and subtract the length that will be added by the endcap. Keep in mind your braid will fit partly inside the endcap. My endcap is 1" long, but I can see the wells are ¼" deep on each end. That means the endcap will only add ½" to the length of my bracelet. I'll subtract ½" from my 6½" wrist measurement and get 6". That means my goal for the braided length of my bracelet will be 6". Multiply your braided length by three and add 1½" for waste. In my case, I need to make a braid 19½" long.

Set Up

For each of the 16 spools of beading wire, remove the spool clip and let out about a foot of wire. Replace the spool clip. Tie the 16 ends of wire together using an overhand knot. Follow the starting diagram for color placement **(a)**.

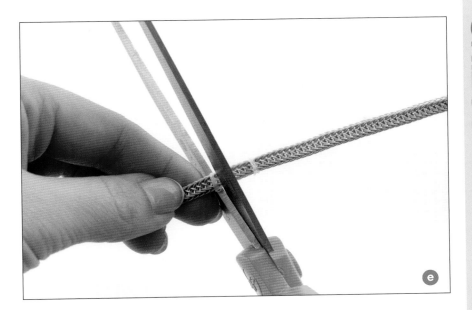

There's a kink in my wire!

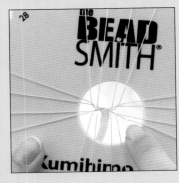

It's OK. Just keep braiding. A little kink will be almost invisible in the braid. It took me a long time to find it here on my braid so I could show you, and I knew where to look!

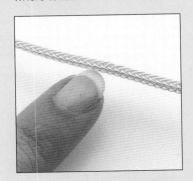

Lock the wires in place on the double-thick kumihimo disk using the standard starting position for a trapezoid braid (see p. 95). Clip the center weight below the knot, trying to clip as many of the wires as possible **(b)**.

Clipping the wires together helps to prevent the knot from untying itself. If needed, use a bead stopper in addition to the center weight to clip the wires together.

Braiding
Braid using the 16-warp trapezoid-braid sequence (see p. 95). You'll need to periodically remove the spool clips and let out more wire. Braid until you've reached your desired length.

Finishing
On top of the disk, slide a hemostat between the wires and the disk **(c)**.

Clamp the braid at the point of braiding. Remove the braid from the disk and bind near the hemostat. Keep the binding as small and flat as possible. Glue the bind with Hypo Cement, making sure to glue all sides of the binding **(d)**.

Also generously glue the braid itself on the "cut side" of the binding. The wire has a lot of spring-back and the binding alone won't hold the braid together. Trim the excess wire about 2" from the hemostat.

Referring to your earlier measurements, make a second binding a bracelet length away from the first binding. In my case, the bindings are 6" apart. Move down ½" and bind again. Move down a bracelet length and bind again. Make two more bindings this way so you have bound both ends of three bracelet length sections. Double-check your measurements and make sure every section is exactly the same length!

When you are happy with the bindings, glue each one with Hypo Cement and put some extra cement on the braid where you'll make the cuts. Allow to dry at least 60 minutes or until the glue is no longer tacky. Cut the braid into the three segments using sharp, heavy-duty craft scissors **(e)**.

TIP
Don't use your good kumihimo scissors on the wire! You'll ruin the scissors.

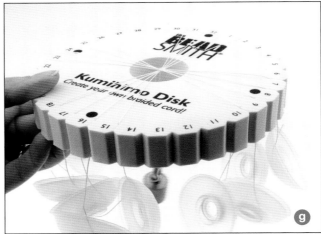

Kumihimo Math

Working from the mini 10' spools of beading wire is a very convenient way to approach this project. You don't have to transfer the wire to bobbins, and you don't have to do any measuring to get started—but now that you've made one of these awesome bracelets, you're probably wondering if you have enough wire left over to make a second.

To calculate your usage multiplier for this project, measure the remaining wire on one of the spools to determine how much you used for the bracelet. I started with 10' mini spools and I have about 7¼' remaining on each spool. That means I used 2¾' of wire per warp. I'm going to round it up to 3'. My total finished braid length was 23". (Yes, I braided more than I needed.) Take the amount of wire used per warp (36" in my case) and divide that by the length of the braid (23") and you get 1.57. That's the usage multiplier. We can use that to estimate how much wire is needed per warp.

Let's say we want to make a bracelet to fit an 8" wrist. Following the instructions in the "Kumihimo Math" section, p. 14, we know we need a braid 24" long. Multiply 24 x 1.57 and you get 37.68". Let's round that up to 38". You'll need 38" of wire per warp to make an 8" bracelet.

Cut as close to the bindings as you can without cutting the bindings off. Use a toothpick to line the inside of the magnetic endcap with E6000 glue. Stick the braids in one at a time so they lay side by side inside the endcap **(f)**.

It's a very tight fit, so be patient and use a clean toothpick as a poker, if necessary. Wait until the first end of the bracelet is completely dry, then repeat for the other end of the bracelet.

Alternative Starting Method

If you don't have 16 mini spools of beading wire available, you can still make this project by cutting the needed lengths from 30' or 100' spools. Refer to the sizing chart to determine your warp length and cut eight pieces of wire that length.

Wrist Size	Total Braid Length	Warp length for "no-knot start"
6½"	19½"	62"
7"	21"	66"
7½"	22½"	72"
8"	24"	74"

Set up the disk using a "no-knot start" and use plain bobbins to contain the wire instead of mini spools **(g)**.

Mixed Messages
DESIGNING WITH MULTIPLE BRAIDS

Multistrand necklaces and bracelets are a beautiful way to show off some of the new braids you've learned. The possibilities with design are endless! You can really use any combination of braid structures and colors.

On the Vine
Necklace

By making the two braids separately and then sewing them together, you have the freedom to play with the layout and design while everything is in the pinning stage. Get things just the way you want before you start sewing it all together. This project combines eight-warp basketweave and eight-warp half-round.

➤ **Supply List**

Kumihimo Toolkit
- standard thickness disk
- **8** plain bobbins
- 90g center weight
- #10 beading needle
- sewing pins

Other Materials
- 12 yd. 2mm hand-dyed satin cord
- 12 yd. 3mm flat tube ribbon (such as Veragata or Isuki)
- pendant with 4–5mm bail
- beading thread in a color to match the flat tube ribbon
- 8mm endcap
- lobster-claw claw (or clasp of choice)
- **2** small jump rings to attach the clasp

Finished Necklace Length: 18½"

Set Up and Braiding

Use the satin cord to make an eight-warp basketweave braid (see p. 17). Use a "no-knot start" to maximize your length. You need at least 20" of braid for the necklace, but just braid until you run out of cord. When you're finished, remove the braid from the disk and knot the end. Don't cut the ends or glue on endcaps yet.

Use the flat tube ribbon to make an eight-warp half-round braid (see p. 45). Use a "no-knot start" to maximize your length. You need at least 30" for the necklace, but just keep braiding until you run out of cord. Remove the braid from the disk and knot the end. Don't cut the ends or glue on endcaps yet.

Pinning

Slide the "no-knot start" end of the half round braid (HR) through the pendant. Center the pendant (a).

Hold the HR braid against the center of the basketweave braid (BW). Let the pendant hang about ½" below the BW braid. Position the HR braid so that the rounded side is facing the front of the necklace. Pin in place (b).

Make sure the pins go completely through both the HR and BW braids.

TIP

When pinning, always make sure the pin goes all the way through both the HR and the BW. In the case of a full wrap, the pin needs to go through the HR on the front of the necklace, the BW, and the HR on the back of the necklace.

Starting on one side of the pendant, wrap the HR around the BW three times. Keep the rounded side of the HR facing out. When the third wrap is completed, the HR should be under the

BW with the loose end pointing down towards the pendant. Pin in place (c).

Repeat on the other side of the necklace (d).

TIP

Because we want this necklace to be symmetrical, it is important to measure frequently. These instructions will tell you to do something to one side of the necklace and then to do the same thing to the other side. Every time you finish the second side, check your measurements.

On one side of the necklace, loosely wrap the HR from the front of the necklace over and round the BW, traveling about 2". Pin in place with the flat side of the HR touching the BW. The HR should finish under the BW, with the loose end pointing down towards the pendant (e).

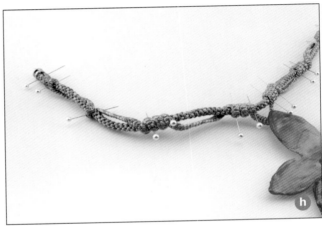

Do the same on the other side of the necklace.

On one side of the necklace, wrap the HR around the BW three times. Keep the wraps right next to each other. Pin in place with the flat side of the HR touching the BW. The HR should finish under the BW with the loose end pointing down towards the pendant. Do the same on the other side of the necklace **(f)**.

TIP
It takes about 1" of HR to make one complete wrap around the BW.

On one side of the necklace, loosely wrap the HR from the front of the necklace over and around the BW, traveling about 2". Pin in place with the flat side of the HR touching the BW **(g)**.

The HR should make one complete wrap around the BW, finishing on top of the BW with the loose end pointing up away from the pendant. Do the same on the other side of the necklace.

On one side of the necklace, loosely wrap the HR from the back of the necklace over and around the BW, traveling about 2". Pin in place. Wrap the HR around the BW a second time. Pin in place. Place the remaining HR parallel to the BW and pin in place. Repeat on the other side of the necklace **(h)**.

Check your work! Make sure it is even on both sides. Make sure the pendant is centered. If the HR tail is longer on one side than the other, don't worry about it. We'll cut the excess off later.

When I lay out my necklace and measure end to end, I get 16". That means the bail of my pendant should be at the 8" mark (i).

Sewing

Each wrap of the HR needs to be sewn to the BW. It is important the thread closely matches the color of the HR.

Starting at the center of the necklace and then alternating sides, do the following for each group of wraps or single wrap:

Start a new thread and make a double or triple knot at the end. Hide the knot and make several anchoring stitches. If there are multiple wraps in the group, transition to the next wrap and make more anchoring stitches. Remove the pins as each section is secured. End the thread.

Hide the knot: Cut 18" of thread and thread a sharp needle. Make a double knot at the end of the thread and trim off any tail. Starting at the center of the necklace in one of the three-wrap groupings on either the right or the left of the pendant, position the needle between the HR and the BW. Sew up through the HR. Try to sew through a "low spot" in the center of the braid (j). Pull the thread through until the knot is against the HR.

Anchoring stitches: Turn around and sew back into the HR braid in pretty much the exact same place as where the thread is coming out (k). By entering and exiting in the same place, you are making the smallest possible stitch on the surface of the HR braid.

Continue pushing the needle into the BW and into the HR that is on the back of the necklace. The needle should exit through a low spot in the HR. Make as many stitches as required to secure the wrap. Remove pins when each section is secure.

Transition to the adjacent wrap: To move from one wrap to the next, sew back into the HR braid in pretty much the exact same place as where the thread is coming out. Push the needle through the BW at an angle so it exits through a low spot in the adjacent wrap of HR (l).

End the thread: Sew back into the HR braid in the same low spot the thread is coming from, but this time don't push into the BW. We're just sewing through the HR **(m)**.

Pull the thread all the way through. Working on the back of the HR, between the HR and the BW, sew through a tiny bit of just the underside of the HR **(n)**.

Pull the thread slowly through until there is only a small loop of it remaining. Before this loop closes, sew through the loop **(o)**.

Pull the thread to close the loop and make a knot. The knot will be on the underside of the HR between the HR and the BW. Trim the tail close.

Finishing: Both braids will go into the endcap, so at your desired endpoints, bind the braids together. Whip stitch the bindings **(p)**. For each end of the necklace, cut off the excess braid very close to the binding and glue on an endcap.

Sampler
Necklace

For my necklace, I wanted each braid to have a slightly different color scheme, but to still be unified with the overall color palette for the necklace. I chose plum as the main color and used it for four warps in each braid. Then I chose four different shades of blue and used them in different combinations in each braid. You could also try making each braid the same color or each braid a different solid color. Have fun playing with this one! Just keep in mind, if you make changes to the number or type of braids in your design, you may need a different size endcap. This piece uses eight-warp basketweave, half-round, and square braids.

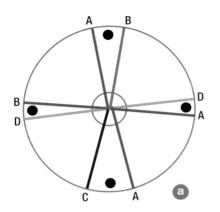

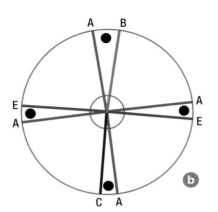

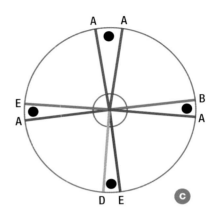

Set Up and Braiding

Following the starting diagrams, make one eight-warp square braid (see p. 80), one eight-warp basketweave braid (see p. 17), and one eight-warp half-round braid (see p. 45) **(a, b, c)**.

Bind the square braid to your desired length for the shortest strand of the necklace. Bind the basketweave braid 1" longer than the square braid. Bind the half-round braid 1" longer than the basketweave braid. Binding each strand of the necklace 1" longer than the strand above it will allow the braids to hang nicely with a little space in between them. If you prefer more space between the strands, try a 2" difference in length. For the example necklace, the square braid is 17½", the basketweave is 18½", and the half-round is 19½".

Stack the braids (aligning the bindings) so the basketweave is on top of the flat side of the half-round braid and the square braid is on top of the basketweave braid. Bind the three braids together **(d)**.

Stack and bind the braids in the same way for the other side of the necklace. Make sure none of the braids are twisted together and everything hangs the way you want it to **(e)**.

If it doesn't, carefully snip the binding and try again. Once you're happy with the bindings, whip stitch to secure (see p. 114). Carefully trim the excess braid close to the binding. You may need to trim each braid separately. Glue an endcap on each end of the necklace and allow to dry for 24 hours. Use jump rings to attach a clasp.

➤ **Supply List**

Kumihimo Toolkit
- standard thickness disk
- **8** plain bobbins
- **90g** center weight

Other Materials
- 1mm satin cord
  - 18 yd. color A
  - 6 yd. color B
  - 3 yd. color C
  - 4½ yd. color D
  - 4½ yd. color E
- **2** 10mm endcaps
- clasp of your choice
- **2** small jump rings

Finished Necklace Length:
approx. 18½"

Sunset
by the Lake
Bracelet

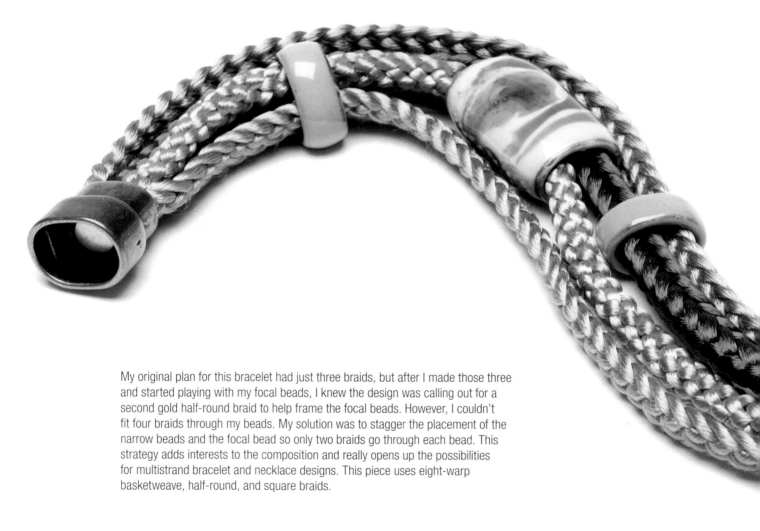

My original plan for this bracelet had just three braids, but after I made those three and started playing with my focal beads, I knew the design was calling out for a second gold half-round braid to help frame the focal beads. However, I couldn't fit four braids through my beads. My solution was to stagger the placement of the narrow beads and the focal bead so only two braids go through each bead. This strategy adds interests to the composition and really opens up the possibilities for multistrand bracelet and necklace designs. This piece uses eight-warp basketweave, half-round, and square braids.

➤ Supply List

Kumihimo Toolkit
- standard thickness disk
- **8** plain bobbins
- 90g center weight

Other Materials
- 1mm rattail
  - 16' color A
  - 32' color B
  - 16' 2mm rattail, color C
- **2** narrow slider beads (11x7mm inside diameter)
- 11x7mm inside diameter focal bead
- **2** 10.2x7mm magnetic endcaps

Finished Bracelet Length:
approx. 7½" (fits 7" wrist)

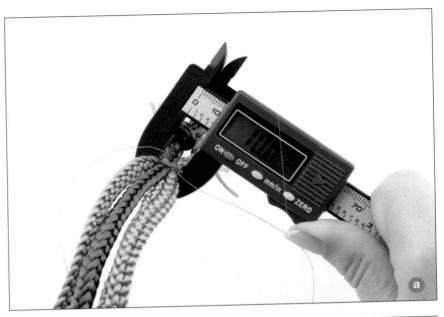

Set Up and Braiding

Cut the satin cord into 24" pieces. Make four separate solid-color braids: one color A eight-warp basketweave braid (see p. 16), two color B eight-warp half-round braids (see p. 44), and one color C eight-warp square braid (see p. 60). Stack the four braids in the following order: one half-round braid, flat side up, then the basketweave braid on top of the half-round, then the square on top of the basketweave. Finally, place the other half-round braid on top of the stack, flat-side down. Tightly bind all four braids together about ¼" from the start of the braids **(a)**.

Use calipers to make sure your binding is tight enough to fit inside your endcaps. Whip stitch the binding to secure (see p. 114) and trim the tails.

Slide one of the narrow beads over the bottom half-round braid and the basketweave braid. I was able to slide the knots at the ends of the braids through my bead, but if you can't, just bind the ends of the braids individually and untie the overhand knot at the end of the braids. Slide the focal bead over the basketweave braid and the square braid. Slide the last narrow slider bead over the square braid and the top half-round braid **(b)**.

Bind the four braids together at your desired length and whip stitch to secure. Cut off the excess braid and glue a magnetic endcap to each end of the bracelet. Allow to dry for 24 hours.

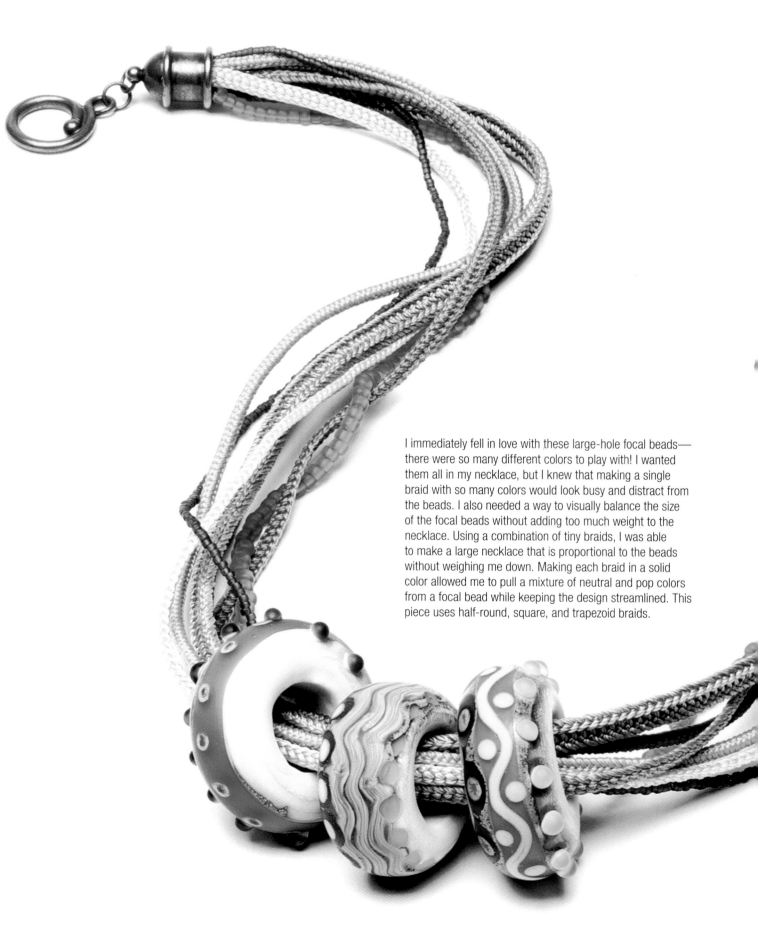

I immediately fell in love with these large-hole focal beads—there were so many different colors to play with! I wanted them all in my necklace, but I knew that making a single braid with so many colors would look busy and distract from the beads. I also needed a way to visually balance the size of the focal beads without adding too much weight to the necklace. Using a combination of tiny braids, I was able to make a large necklace that is proportional to the beads without weighing me down. Making each braid in a solid color allowed me to pull a mixture of neutral and pop colors from a focal bead while keeping the design streamlined. This piece uses half-round, square, and trapezoid braids.

Mighty Micro
Braids
Necklace

➤ Supply List

Kumihimo Toolkit
- double-thickness disk
- **16** plain bobbins
- 90g center weight
- #10 beading needle
- big-eye needle
- thimble (optional)

Other Materials
- size 18 nylon string
  - 12 yd. in each of **4** colors (A, B, C, and D)
  - 24 yd. color E
- 60" micro string
- 6–8g 8° seed beads
- 2–3g 15° seed beads
- **3** focal beads with minimum 12mm inside diameter
- **2** 8mm magnetic endcaps

Finished Necklace Length:
approx. 19½"

Set Up and Braiding

Make five necklace length braids using size 18 nylon string. You're welcome to use any combination of braid structures you like, but keep in mind if you change the recipe, you may need to change your endcap size. Here's what's in my necklace:
- Two eight-warp square braids (see p. 60) (chartreuse and mahogany)
- Two eight-warp half-round braids (see p. 44) (natural and gold)
- One 16-warp trapezoid braid (see p. 94) (khaki)

Bind all five braids together at each end, making sure the distance between the bindings is equal to your desired finished length minus the clasp length. My bindings are 18" apart. Don't cut the thread tails. Use the longer binding thread tail and the #10 beading needle to whip stitch the binding to the braids (see p. 114). This will ensure one braid can't work its way out of the endcap.

TIP
It can be tough to push the needle through the dense braids. Save your fingers and use a thimble.

Add the Seed Beads
Cut a piece of micro string to your necklace length plus 12". Working below the binding, separate the braids and use the big-eye needle to pull the micro string up between the braids, leaving a 6" tail **(a)**.

Anchor the micro string to the binding by sewing up between the braids two more times **(b)**.

Take a stitch down through the binding so the micro string is pointing away from the braid tails that will be cut off **(c)**.

Use the big-eye needle to string a length of 15º seed beads ¼" shorter than your braids. Anchor the micro string to the other binding in the same way as before. When anchoring the micro string, leave a tiny bit of slack on the line **(d)**. You want the beads to fall about ⅛" below the bindings. This helps the seed beads drape better.

Run the micro string back through the 15ºs and tie a half-hitch knot to secure. Continue running the micro string through the 15ºs a few more beads, and then trim the tail **(e)**.

Repeat with the tail thread on the other side of the necklace.

Add a second string of beads using the same method, but this time use 8º seed beads. You can play with the placement of this second string of beads. It doesn't have to be right next to the first string.

Finishing

Use your best scissors to carefully snip off the excess braid beyond the bindings, one braid at a time **(f)**. Add the focal beads and then glue on endcaps. Allow to dry for 24 hours. Use jump rings to attach the clasp.

Design Idea

Do you have focal beads in your stash that have smaller holes? This concept will still work. Put one micro braid through the focal beads and arrange the other braids so they hang above and below the beads.

Marudai

Kumihimo Disk versus Marudai

Traditionally, kumihimo is done using a wooden braiding stand called a marudai.

A marudai consists of a round, smooth piece of wood with a hole in the middle (called a mirror), four wooden legs, and a square wooden base. The fibers you're braiding with are wrapped around wooden, weighted bobbins called *tama*. To counter the weight of the tama, you hang weights from the braid.

I love braiding on my marudai! It's super-fast because you use both hands at the same time and you reposition the warps by sliding. You also have more control over the tension in the braid because you get to play with the center weights. So, why isn't this book about braiding on a marudai?

There is a big intimidation factor when it comes to learning how to use a marudai. It's sad to admit, but my own marudai sat unused for over a year when I first bought it because I just didn't know

where to start and kept putting it off. Marudai can also be difficult to come by. These things aren't being cranked out on factory assembly lines. Each one is made by a skilled carpenter and that takes time. There are very few stores that carry them. Once you do find one, they're on the pricey side, owing to the cost of quality materials and skilled craftsmanship.

The foam kumihimo disk, on the other hand, is very inexpensive and readily obtainable. Pretty much every bead store sells them these days. I learned kumihimo on the disk and that's how I like to teach my beginning students.

For those of you looking to expand your kumihimo repertoire, I've included a marudai quick-start guide and braid diagrams for the three eight-warp structures covered in this book.

Marudai *Quick-Start Guide*

Set Up

My favorite way to start a marudai braid is with a variation of a "no-knot start." Take the number of warps in the braid and divide by two. This is how many pieces of cord you'll cut. Take the warp length and multiply by two. That's how long to cut each piece. For example, let's say I'm making an eight-warp basketweave braid and I want the warps to be 1½ yd. each. To set up on the marudai, I'll cut four 3-yd. pieces of cord. Line up the ends of the cords and fold them in half to find the middle. So far this is just like a "no-knot start." Here's where

we change it up for the marudai: Tie the folded cords in a knot, leaving a small loop **(a)**.

We'll use this loop later as a place to hang our center weights. This is my preferred marudai start method because as the center weights pull down on the braid, the knot tightens, ensuring even slippery fibers like satin hold securely and the weight can't fall off.

Slide the chopstick through the fiber loop and center it. Drop the chopstick down through the hole in the mirror.

➤ Supply List

Kumihimo Toolkit
- 3mm satin cord
  - 6 yd. color A
  - 6 yd. color B
- marudai
- chopstick
- painter's tape
- **8** 70g tama
- S-hook
- **6** 23g washers
- metal shower curtain ring

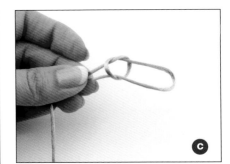

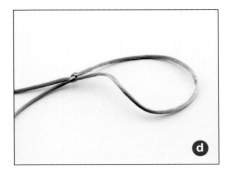

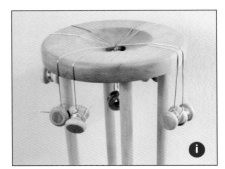

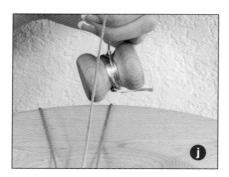

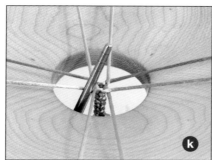

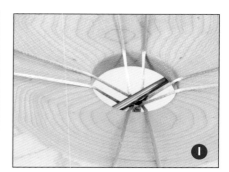

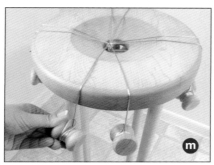

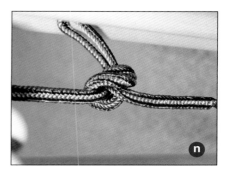

Use two pieces of painter's tape to secure the chopstick to the underside of the mirror. The warps should be hanging above the mirror **(b)**.

Tie a slipknot at the end of each warp: make a loop with the end of the warp like you're going to tie an overhand knot, but instead of bringing the tail through the loop, pull the long side through the loop **(c)**. Tighten **(d)**.

Wind each warp onto a tama: Slide the slip-knot onto the center of the tama and tighten. Wind the warp around the tama so that the warp is coming off the bottom of the tama. Hold the tama in your non-dominant hand keeping tension on the warp. Place your dominant hand palm-down on the warp **(e)**.

Flip your dominant hand over, pulling a loop of warp around your hand as you do so **(f)**.

The hand holding the tama is only moving enough to keep up with the warp as you pull it around your other hand. Don't flip the tama. With your knuckles brushing the tama, slide the loop onto the center of the tama **(g)**. Pull your fingers out of the loop and let go of the tama.

Keep all of the tama on the same side of the marudai until you have all eight wound **(h)**. Then arrange the tama in the starting position for your braid.

Slide the S-hook into the loop with the chop stick. Put six washers onto the metal show curtain ring and hang them from the s-hook. Remove the painter's tape and the chopstick **(i)**.

Now you're ready to braid.

Braiding on the Marudai

We'll move two warps simultaneously when braiding on the marudai. That's where the speed advantage comes from. Follow along with the braiding diagrams to get started. Notice the left-hand and right-hand are indicated for each step. When moving the warps, lift the warp onto your fingers without pinching the cord or cupping the tama **(j)**. It's important the tama can hang freely to ensure even tension.

Try to complete an entire sequence without stopping so you don't lose your place. When you need to stop, use the chopstick as a parking break: Starting below the mirror, bring the chopstick up through the hole on one side of the braid **(k)**.

Cross over the braid with the chopstick and lock the end of the chopstick below the mirror **(l)**.

This will stabilize the braid and make it less likely to shift and slide if your marudai gets bumped.

As you work, you'll need to release more cord from the tama from time to time. Gently rotate the tama so that the loop loosens and pull downward to release more cord **(m)**.

As the braid gets longer, tie knots as necessary to keep the waits from resting on the bottom of the stand **(n)**.

When finished braiding, remove the center weights. Hold the braid above the mirror at the point of braid and lift everything off of the marudai. Knot or bind the end of the braid and then remove the tama.

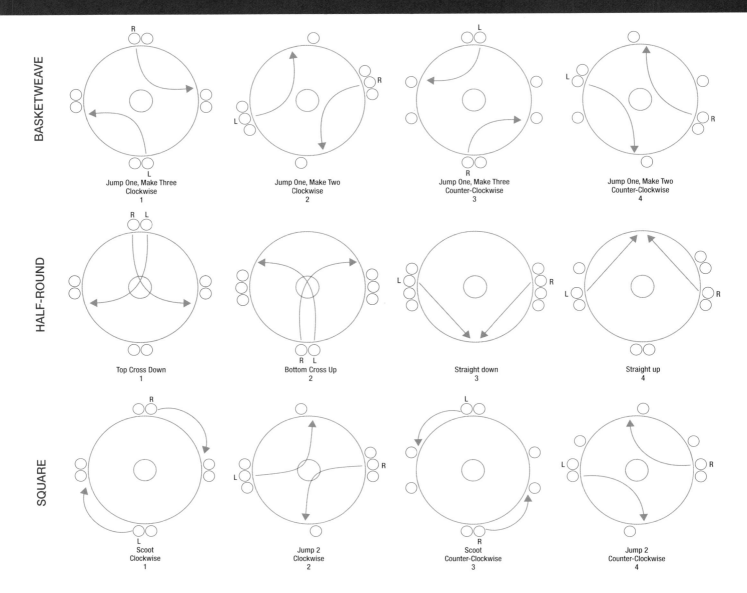

BASKETWEAVE

Jump One, Make Three
Clockwise
1

Jump One, Make Two
Clockwise
2

Jump One, Make Three
Counter-Clockwise
3

Jump One, Make Two
Counter-Clockwise
4

HALF-ROUND

Top Cross Down
1

Bottom Cross Up
2

Straight down
3

Straight up
4

SQUARE

Scoot
Clockwise
1

Jump 2
Clockwise
2

Scoot
Counter-Clockwise
3

Jump 2
Counter-Clockwise
4

Controlling Tension with Center Weights

How many center weights you need will depend on the materials you're braiding with and how many tama you're using. You have a lot of freedom to play with the tension of the braid by adjusting how many center weights you use. Keep in mind, the heavier the center weight, the looser the braid. Try to keep the point of braiding so it is pulling down slightly into the well (the carved out center portion of the mirror), but not pulling into the hole.

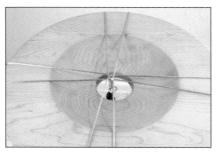

Zero weights. The point of braiding is floating above the mirror and braiding will be difficult.

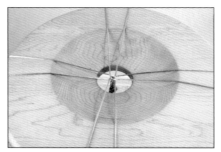

Six weights. The point of braiding is pulling down slightly into the well, but not into the hole. This is ideal tension for most braids.

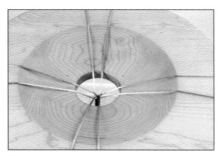

12 weights. The point of braiding is pulling down into the well. This will make an extremely loose braid.

Acknowledgments

I'd like to say *Domo arigato gozaimasu* to my friends Mike Harris and Hiroe Tanabe for their help understanding the Japanese names of braids.

Thank you to all of my students for enthusiastically testing out new projects and giving your feedback. I design with you in mind!

To my husband and partner, Richard Swanborg, thank you for running all those extra miles so I could write in peace!

Thank you to my team at Design & Adorn! We're changing the world, one braider at a time!

I also want to thank everyone on the Kalmbach publishing and marketing team! Thanks for helping make this second book a success!

About the Author

Rebecca's passion for learning and teaching has taken her on adventures around the world. In 2006 she made her home in Tucson, Arizona where she founded Design & Adorn Beading Studio and KumihimoStore.com. She specializes in teaching kumihimo on the disk and marudai and leads a variety of classes and workshops at her shop and venues around the country. When she's not teaching, writing, or running her store, you'll find her enjoying afternoon tea with her husband or off somewhere in search of adventure.

Braid, Knot, & Crochet
Beautiful Jewelry!

Easy-to-follow instructions and photos help you learn new techniques and make jewelry pieces you'll love to wear.

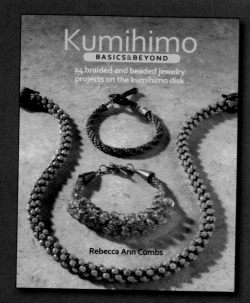